Inequality, Economic Growth and Business Decision-Making

It is now widely recognised that rising inequality of income and wealth on the one hand and a slowdown in the rate of economic growth on the other are two of the most important challenges faced today by the global economy as well as by most of the developing economies. This book starts by explaining how these two issues are interrelated. There is no dearth of books on the role that the economic policies of the government can play in meeting these twin challenges. The role of business managers in the private sector of the economy, however, is a relatively neglected area. This book seeks to close this gap in the literature. The central message of the book is that, contrary to popular belief, it is in the interests of private business itself that business managers take into account the effects that their decisions have on the economy as a whole. It is shown that a failure to do so would hurt their own economic prospects in both the short run and the long. Emphasis is given on the importance of an appropriate orientation of managerial decisions and on the role of investors (i.e. the suppliers of capital) in inducing managers to take socially optimal decisions. The book is addressed as much to business managers and students in management courses as to the general reader. Therefore, no prior knowledge of advanced economic theory is presumed. All arguments are built from first principles.

Asis Kumar Banerjee, former Vice-Chancellor and former Professor of Economics, University of Calcutta, has held visiting positions at Presidency College, Calcutta; Indian Statistical Institute, New Delhi; and University of California, Riverside, California. His research interests include development economics, welfare economics, game theory and the measurement of inequality and poverty. His previous publications include the books *Measuring Development: An Inequality Dominance Approach* (2020) and *Economic Slowdown in India: An Introductory Analysis* (2023).

Routledge Focus on Management and Society
Series Editor: Anindya Sen
Pro Vice-Chancellor, School of Social Sciences, Ramaiah University of Applied Sciences, India

The aim of the Focus series is to present the reader with a number of short volumes which deal with important managerial issues in the Indian context. Volumes already published in the series cover topics which are of perennial interest to managers, like strategic change and transformation, and supply chain management, as well as emerging areas of research like neuromarketing and digital culture. CEOs today also need to be familiar with critical developments in other fields, like auction theory and the contribution of sociology to management thinking. A forthcoming volume examines the law of one price in the context of dually listed shares, that is, shares which are listed in both Indian stock markets and abroad. In other words, the Focus series is designed to introduce management theorists and researchers (as well as the general public) to a diverse set of topics relevant directly or peripherally to management in a short, readable format, without sacrificing basic rigour and set in the Indian context.

Artificial Intelligence, Business and Civilization
Our Fate Made in Machines
Andreas Kaplan

Law of One Price
A Chronicle of Dually Listed Indian Stocks
Vinodh Madhavan and Partha Ray

Indian Gold Jewellery Industry
Culture and Consumption
Sylvia Raha

Inequality, Economic Growth and Business Decision-Making
Asis Kumar Banerjee

For more information about this series, please visit: www.routledge.com/
Routledge-Focus-on-Management-and-Society/book-series/RFMS

Inequality, Economic Growth and Business Decision-Making

Asis Kumar Banerjee

Routledge
Taylor & Francis Group

LONDON AND NEW YORK

First published 2025
by Routledge
4 Park Square, Milton Park, Abingdon, Oxon OX14 4RN

and by Routledge
605 Third Avenue, New York, NY 10158

Routledge is an imprint of the Taylor & Francis Group, an informa business

British Library Cataloguing-in-Publication Data
A catalogue record for this book is available from the British Library

Library of Congress Cataloging-in-Publication Data
Names: Banerjee, Asis K., author.
Title: Inequality, economic growth and business decision-making /
Asis Kumar Banerjee.
Description: Abingdon, Oxon ; New York, NY : Routledge, 2025. |
Series: Routledge focus on management and society | Includes
bibliographical references and index. |
Identifiers: LCCN 2024020458 (print) | LCCN 2024020459 (ebook) |
ISBN 9781032707068 (hardback) | ISBN 9781032707075 (paperback) |
ISBN 9781032707082 (ebook)
Subjects: LCSH: Economic policy. | Income distribution. | Economic
development.
Classification: LCC HD87 .B36 2025 (print) | LCC HD87 (ebook) |
DDC 338.9--dc23/eng/20240531
LC record available at https://lccn.loc.gov/2024020458
LC ebook record available at https://lccn.loc.gov/2024020459

ISBN: 978-1-032-70706-8 (hbk)
ISBN: 978-1-032-70707-5 (pbk)
ISBN: 978-1-032-70708-2 (ebk)

DOI: 10.4324/9781032707082

Typeset in Times New Roman
by SPi Technologies India Pvt Ltd (Straive)

In memoriam
Anjan Banerjee

Contents

Tables

Preface

There are two quite different reasons why one may be interested in matters relating to economic inequality. One of these is essentially a subjective value judgement that considers a high degree of inequality to be morally revolting. The other is related to the *economic* consequences of inequality. As is the case with many other inequality researchers, my own interest in the matter had its origin in the first of these two motivations. I considered inequality to be unethical and, therefore, concluded that every effort should be made to minimise it. To understand how effective these efforts are, however, we need to decide, in the first place, how to *measure* inequality. Since then, I have spent a lot of time trying to understand the measurement issues in this context. I have learned (I hope) a few things about them and I am still learning.

Over the years, however, I have come to feel that as a student of economics I should also be concerned with the question how inequality affects the economy, especially, how, if at all, it affects the rate of economic *growth*. I found that while there was no unanimous answer to the question in the academic literature, the balance of evidence tilted towards the hypothesis that, at least in the less-developed economies and at least in the long run (if not also in the short), an increase in inequality reduced the growth rate. It is hardly necessary to emphasise that the task of boosting the rate of growth has a degree of urgency in *all* developing economies (including the relatively fast-growing ones such as India). Since inequality has a negative effect on the growth rate, the task of reducing inequality assumes urgency not only from the viewpoint of the moral philosopher but also from that of the hard-nosed economist. Sharing this understanding with the reader has been a major motivation for me in writing the present book.

Traditionally, it is the government's redistributive policies (such as taxes on the rich and transfers to the poor) that are considered to be the main instruments for reducing economic inequality. Over the last few decades, however, almost all of the economies have undergone a process of *privatisation* which has de-emphasised the role of the government in general. As is well-known, this is a part of the broader process of *globalisation* and the move towards the adoption of the neoliberal economic philosophy. Be that as it may, what is relevant for us here is that it has considerably blunted the instruments of redistributive government policies. Moreover, even before privatisation became fashionable, it had always been the case that governments in the less-developed economies faced severe resource limitations in carrying out its pro-poor transfer programmes. For obvious reasons, a poor country has a poor government.

How, then, do we go about reducing inequality? In this book, I have argued, somewhat unconventionally, that under the circumstances it is the private business sector of the economy that can (and, indeed, must) play an active role. The reader may, at first, find the suggestion quite puzzling. In fact, in popular discourses on inequality the blame for the prevailing high degree of inequality in the world today is almost routinely laid at the doors of profit policies of business firms. It is not my intention to suggest that this conventional position on the matter is totally unacceptable. I do suggest, however, that it misses some vital points. In particular, it is commonsense that business flourishes in a growing economy and stagnates in a sluggish one. Recent academic research also lends support to the hypothesis that the growth rate of the economy has a positive effect on business performance. Now, recall what was said above about the effect of inequality on growth. If rising inequality causes a growth slowdown and if the latter, in turn, has a deleterious effect on the performance of business firms, it follows that it is in the interests of the business sector to join hands in the society's efforts to reduce inequality.

Note that this, again, is a hard-nosed economic argument. It is not a call for a "change of hearts" on the part of business managers. On the contrary, as I have tried to show in the book, it urges managers to engage in *rational* decision-making. I have emphasised, however, that *true* rationality must be distinguished from what merely masquerades as rationality. This is the basic message of this book.

Writing this book has been an educative process for me as it has helped me understand the many nuances of rational business decision-making and their relations with the issue of inequality. Throughout the process, I have had the opportunity of discussing my ideas with a number of economists. I am indebted to Amitabha Bose, Dipankar Dasgupta, Pradip Maiti, Mihir Rakshit, Susmita Rakshit and Soumyen Sikdar among others for their incisive comments. I have also benefitted from the observations made by the participants in seminars given by me at various places (such as the Indian Statistical Institute, the Indian Institute of Management Calcutta and Calcutta University) on topics that were closely related to the subject of this book.

The book belongs to the Routledge Focus on Management and Society series, and I am indebted to Anindya Sen, the Series Editor, for his detailed comments on the initial draft of the manuscript.

Thanks are also due to Towfeeq Wani, Editor, Routledge, for guiding me through the entire process from formulating the book proposal to submitting the final version of the manuscript.

Kolkata,
December, 2023
Asis Kumar Banerjee

Abbreviations

AC	Average Cost
AI	Artificial Intelligence
AIDIS	All India Debt and Investment Survey
BCG	Boston Consultancy Group
BRICS	Brazil, Russia, India, China and South Africa
CSR	Corporate Social Responsibility
GDP	Gross Domestic Product
GOI	Government of India
HBS	Household Balance Sheet
HCMC	Human Capital Management Coalition
IBEF	Indian Brand Equity Foundation
IHDS	Indian Human Development Survey
IT	Information Technology
MBA	Master of Business Administration
MC	Marginal Cost
MRP	Mixed Recall Period
NCAER	National Council of Applied Economic Research
NITI	National Institution for Transforming India
NSO	National Statistical Office
NSSO	National Sample Survey Office
NSTC	National Science and Technology Council
OECD	Organisation for Economic Cooperation and Development
PPP	Purchasing Power Parity
PRI	Principles of Responsible Investment
RBI	Reserve Bank of India
SDGs	Social Development Goals
TCFD	Task Force on Climate-related Financial Disclosures
TIFD	Task Force on Inequality-related Financial Disclosures
TIIP	The Investment Integration Project
TSFD	Task Force on Social-related Financial Disclosures

UN	United Nations
UNDP	United Nations Development Programme
URP	Uniform Recall Period
WBCSD	World Business Council for Sustainable Development
WDI	Workforce Disclosure Initiative
WEF	World Economic Forum
WID	World Inequality Database

1   Prologue

1.1 Introduction: The basic agenda

1.1.1 Inequality

In 2013, the World Economic Forum (WEF) released the results of a survey of 1592 leaders from academia, government, business and non-profit organisations. The survey sought to identify the ten most important trends that faced the world, arranged in decreasing order of importance. Number two on the list was found to be *widening income disparities* among people (see WEF (2013)). Moreover, respondents from many regions of the world (which included Asia) accorded this particular trend the number one position.[1] A 2015 research paper by economists at the International Monetary Fund (IMF) goes so far as to assert, "Widening income inequality is the defining challenge of our time" (see Dabla-Norris et. al. (2015)). For more recent expressions of concern over rising income inequality, see, for instance, Chancel et. al. (2022) and Qureshi (2023).

Needless to say, income inequality is not the only type of inequality. There are many other types of economic and social disparities. Concern over inequality in the broad sense found expression in the Sustainable Development Goals (SDGs) of the United Nations (UN). The UN General Assembly formulated the SDGs in 2015. The SDGs are a collection of 17 interrelated objectives which are intended to serve as a "shared blueprint for peace and prosperity for the people and the planet, now and into the future". The tenth on this list of objectives is "reduced inequalities" (www.sdgs.un.org).

The present book is about inequality. However, while the choice of the subject matter was partly motivated by the widespread concern for this important economic and social problem of our times that has found expression in the references cited above, the book does not aspire to be a comprehensive treatise on the topic of inequality in the broad sense. It focuses exclusively on inequalities of *income* and *wealth*.[2]

DOI: 10.4324/9781032707082-1

1.1.2 Economic growth

Why, however, should one be concerned at all about income (or wealth) inequality? One possible answer to the question would be that it is a value judgement. Inequality is a bad thing per se because it violates our ethical values. It is considered to be inherently unjust. However, it should be noted at the outset that while I do share this ethical or moral sentiment, it is not the principal motivation behind this book. There are grounds for believing that inequality has undesirable *economic* consequences. Specifically, much of this book is concerned with the effect of an increase in inequality on *economic growth*. Other things remaining the same, rising inequality pushes down the growth rate. The need for fast economic growth in an economy such as that of India hardly requires a detailed discussion.

As will be seen in the following chapters, however, the relation between inequality and economic growth is a two-directional one. As we have just said above, inequality has a negative impact on growth, that is, an increase in inequality depresses the growth rate (and, similarly, a decrease in inequality stimulates it). But there is also a causation in the reverse direction, that is, growth has a negative impact on inequality. Other things remaining the same, an increase in the growth rate causes inequality to decline and a decrease in the growth rate pushes up inequality. It should be noted that these are not exact mathematical formulas that would hold under all circumstances and in all countries. There have been exceptions to these rules in some countries over some periods of time. Moreover, there may be time lags before the effects make themselves felt. This is especially true about the effect of inequality on growth. If there is an increase in inequality in this period, its negative effect on growth may be observed in the next period rather than immediately. Nevertheless, these are broad tendencies that are expected to be roughly valid. In particular, they are expected to be mostly true for the developing economies of the present-day world.

Thus, a developing country with an increasing inequality trend faces a *vicious circle* which not only constrains future growth possibilities but also exacerbates any pre-existing inequality. If inequality increases in this period, this will reduce the growth rate either immediately or with a time lag which, in turn, will increase inequality either immediately or with a time lag. Many economists believe that this is the characteristic of economic inequality that is the most worrying. Inequality feeds upon itself. Needless to say, for an economy that needs to grow fast enough in order to solve its myriad economic problems and that faces an increasing trend in inequality, one of the most urgent questions is how to break out of this vicious circle.

At this point, we need to clarify that it is not the intention here to suggest that inequality is the *only* factor that hinders economic growth. Indeed, there is a whole gamut of other factors (including both economic and non-economic ones) that have a bearing on the growth rate of an economy. Had the present book been one on the theory of economic growth or on development economics, its domain of analysis would have to be by far larger. The reason why this book focuses on only one factor that inhibits growth (viz. inequality) is that, as discussed before, the rising trend in inequality is widely considered to be one of the most important features of today's world.

1.1.3 The role of business decision-making

The obvious question that arises at this point is what, if anything, can be done to arrest the rising trend of inequality and, if possible, to reverse it. One line that the discussion can follow from this point onwards relates to the role of economic policies of the *government* in the fight against inequality. As is well-known, the macro- and micro-economic policies of the government (for instance, its monetary, fiscal and trade policies, tax-subsidy policies and various types of direct redistributive measures such as cash transfers to the poor) can play an important role in reducing inequality. Much, however, has been written on how and under what conditions these policies work. By now, indeed, there is a vast literature on these issues. In the Indian context see, for instance, Kundu and Cabrera (2022) and Mahendra Dev (2018). Atkinson (2015) is an authoritative treatment in the general setting.

The present book, however, treads a different path. It focuses on the role that business managers *in the private sector of the economy can* play in this context. We argue, somewhat unconventionally, that *rational* business decision-making can (and, indeed, must) pay attention to the task of minimising inequality in the economy as far as practicable.

The reader may, at first, find the last sentence of the previous paragraph quite mystifying. In fact, in popular discourses it is almost a standard practice to lay the blame for the high degree of economic inequality that exists in an economy at the doors of business firms (or, more specifically, of the people who manage them). It is relentless profit-mongering on the part of the producers of goods and services in the private (as opposed to the public) sector of the economy that is alleged to be responsible for the existing state of affairs. How, then, does one expect *rational* business managers to be interested in reducing inequality? Doesn't rationality require business decision-makers to maximise profits?

This book argues that while the popular perception of the role of business firms in perpetrating inequality in the economy may not be completely devoid of truth, it represents an oversimplification of the matter. While rationality certainly implies profit maximisation, it is important for a business firm to pay attention to (a) the long-run sustainability of its profits and (b) the interests of the private business sector of the economy *as a whole* which, as will be seen, are not necessarily the same as those of a particular business firm even in the short run. Each business firm needs to take cognisance of these two vital aspects of business decision-making. Indeed, a failure to do so would endanger each firm by jeopardising its own profit prospects. In other words, it is vital for each business manager to ponder the question what *constitutes* rational business decision-making.

1.2 Economic growth and business profits

How is the matter of inequality related to the issue of rationality? Why should a manager whose notion of rationality is sophisticated enough to encompass the considerations mentioned above want to follow business policies that would help in reducing inequality? To answer this question, first recall that rising inequality slows down the pace of economic growth. (This was one half of the vicious circle of high inequality and slow growth that we referred to before). To this we now add another proposition. The other proposition states that in economies such as that of India, *slow growth causes low business performance*. In particular, it causes low rates of business profits. Thus, rising inequality causes a falling rate of growth which causes a worsening of business performance. On the flip side, business flourishes when inequality decreases. This is why a prudent business decision-maker needs to be interested in reducing the high degree of inequality of income and wealth distributions prevailing today in these economies.

Thus, on the one hand, a developing economy urgently needs to break out of the vicious circle of high inequality and sluggish growth and, on the other, business firms in the private sector, in pursuance of their own interests (as distinct from those of the economy as a whole), need to join hands with the rest of the society in finding a way out of the circle. This is a capsule statement of the basic message of this book.

1.3 Preview of the rest of the book

This section is a preview of the rest of the book. Chapter 2 seeks to apprise the reader of the important facts regarding the broad trends of inequality of income and wealth. Both the global and the Indian pictures are presented in a concise manner. The discovery of new sources of data and the use of new techniques of analysis have led to a significant advancement in our knowledge about these trends. It is now acknowledged by most experts that since the 1990s there has been an increase in inequality *within* almost every country although inequality *between* countries has abated to some extent.

Chapter 3 shows that there are *economic* reasons why we are interested in the issue of inequality. It distinguishes between supply and demand-constrained economies and shows that in both types of economies, an increase in inequality has an adverse effect on the rate of economic growth. The existence of a vicious circle between increasing inequality and stagnating growth is also established. In a supply-constrained economy, there is also a *virtuous circle* in the sense that a *fall* in inequality and *rising* growth rate would reinforce each other, at least in the long run. In a demand-constrained economy there is, again, a vicious circle of the type stated above. While the virtuous circle of falling inequality and rising growth rate cannot be proved in general in this case, it would again be operative if the rate of population growth is low enough. Overall, since the importance of growth for an economy such as that of India hardly needs elaboration, there is a case for believing that a reduction in inequality would be desired not only on the moral ground but also on the economic.

Chapter 4 begins the discussion of the role that business managers in the private sector can play in helping an economy such as that of India to break out of the vicious circle of inequality and slow growth. In fact, it goes a step further. It claims that managers not only *can* but also *must* play this role in their own true interests. It is argued that there is an urgent need to make decision-makers in the private sector aware of the fact that going for the "quick buck" is often not only *socially* suboptimal but also suboptimal for the firms. There are two reasons for this. One of these, on which this chapter focuses, is a *supply-side issue*. The point here is that there is a difference between short- and long-run profits. It is shown that business managers often hurt the *long-run* interests of their firms by attempting to maximise *short-run* profits. Such myopic decision-making may bring some immediate monetary gain but reduces long-term profits by increasing inequality and thereby eroding labour standards and decreasing the growth rate of the economy. Growth deceleration is not in the interests of business firms. It jeopardises their own long-term profit prospects.

Chapter 5 shows that there is also a second reason why a business firm's exclusive concentration on the maximisation of its own profits (and complete disregard for what happens to the performance of the private business *sector* of the economy) often turns out to be self-defeating. This has nothing (or, at least, not that much) to do with the short-run-versus-long-run issue discussed in Chapter 4. Rather, it arises from the fact that, for any group of decision-makers, what is rational from the viewpoint of *each* single decision-maker may turn out to be quite irrational from that of the *group* of decision-makers. Thus, while each single business manager may think that he or she is doing the right thing by trying to maximise the short-run profits of the firm, the interests of the business sector as a whole may actually be jeopardised (even in the short run). This is an example of a situation that is known, in game-theoretic parlance, as the Prisoner's Dilemma. We show that this paradox is particularly likely to arise when economic slowdown is largely caused by the problem of *demand deficiency*.

Chapter 6 is the concluding chapter of the book. It starts by briefly discussing two issues that have not been mentioned in the earlier chapters but are likely to make the social aspects of business decision-making even more important in the coming years than they have been in the past. One of these is *global warming* and the other is the rise of *digital technology* in general and *artificial intelligence* in particular. The rest of the chapter is devoted to a review of the possible ways of sensitising business managers about the need to take into account the consequences of their decisions on the economy as a whole. A number of important steps in this direction have already been taken in some of the advanced economies. There is still, however, a long way to go. Moreover, in countries such as India, progress so far has been negligible. The chapter ends by placing the central message of the book in the context of the recent debate over "woke capitalism".

1.4 Conclusion

This introductory chapter concludes by briefly considering a question that sometimes arises in the course of any discussion on inequality. While inequality (of income or wealth) is certainly an important type of *inequity*, it is not the only one. There are many others. One of these that is obviously of very great importance is *poverty*.[3] "Poverty kills", it is said. It can, therefore, be argued that poverty requires even more urgent attention than inequality.

Should this book, then, have focused on poverty rather than on inequality? It is contended that the focus on inequality is well-grounded in the basic purpose of this book discussed above. In particular, the following two points need to be noted.

First, there is no denying the *importance* of the issue of poverty. If it is a question of ranking the economic *problems* of a developing economy in decreasing order of urgency, there is little doubt that poverty should get one of the top positions in the list. No wonder, eradication of poverty does get the very first position in the list of the SDGs of the UN. As mentioned at the very beginning of this chapter, however, among the various *trends* that confront the global economy today, most observers believe that it is *rising* inequality that is one of the greatest causes of worry. The observed trend of *poverty*, on the other hand, is a *decreasing* one in most of the countries of the world (including India), although there is no doubt that there is still a long way to go before we can claim to have eradicated poverty completely from the face of the earth. This is one of the main reasons behind the focus on inequality in this book: inequality is *rising*.

Second, reducing inequality is an effective way of reducing poverty. To see why, note that the most widely used policy intervention for the purpose of poverty reduction takes the form of redistributive programmes of the government such as transfers of cash and other benefits to the poor. In most countries, it is this type of government action that has been the major factor behind the reduction in poverty that has been achieved so far. Obviously, however, the scope of this type of policies is limited by the government's resource limitations. Indeed, if that was not the case, then poverty would have been extinct from the face of the earth by now. It is in this connection that inequality reduction can play an important role. Inequality is a constraint on economic growth in the developing world. A decrease in inequality would push up the growth rate and faster growth of national income would mean faster growth of *government revenue* from taxes and other sources. This will enable the government to increase its expenditure on redistributive programmes. There will also eventually be a beneficial *trickle-down* effect of economic growth on all sections of the society including the poor even though at first it may be only the richer classes that benefit from growth. It may seem that this points towards the need to stimulate the growth rate by *any* available means, not necessarily by reducing inequality. However, the importance of inequality reduction in this context is that *it is usually the more egalitarian economies that tend to have larger trickle-down effects*. There is considerable empirical evidence that the extent to which economic growth reduces *poverty* depends crucially on the degree of *inequality* that prevails in the economy. For instance, a World Bank report considered the strength of the poverty-reducing power of economic growth to be given by the *elasticity of poverty with respect to growth* which is defined to be the percentage reduction in poverty per 1 per cent increase in the rate of economic growth. Poverty was measured by the *head count ratio* (see Note 3). By studying a sample of 62 countries, the report came to the conclusion that the greater the value of this elasticity in a country, the lower was the inequality of the distribution of income in the country (see World Bank (2006, 84–87)).

Some commentators have expressed the apprehension that attempts to reduce inequality by *government actions* would face the same problem of resource limitation as besets the attempts to reduce poverty because the required government actions are quite similar in the two cases and basically consist of income transfers to the low-income groups. Therefore, there is no special advantage in using inequality reduction through government intervention as a way of reducing poverty. I wish to state that I have no disagreement with this argument. On the contrary, it is partly in view of this type of limitation on government actions that this book poses the unconventional question whether rational decision-making by managers in the *private* sector of the economy can have a role in enabling a developing economy to break out of the vicious circle of rising inequality and decelerating growth. This returns us to the basic theme of this book outlined in Section 1.1.

Notes

1 The overall number one was *rising societal tensions in the Middle East and North Africa*. It can be argued, however, that income disparities were, at least partly, responsible for these tensions.
2 Accordingly, throughout the book, the word *inequality* will often be used as a shorthand for the inequality of the distributions of income and wealth among the people of the country.
3 Inequality and poverty are notionally different issues. Inequality (of income) involves a comparison of incomes of different persons. The alternative formulas that have been suggested for measuring inequality differ among themselves regarding the precise ways of making such comparisons and of arriving at an aggregate of these differences. Poverty, however, is essentially an absolute (rather than a relative) concept. A person whose income is below the *poverty line* (i.e. the cost of attaining a specified minimal standard of living) is poor. No comparison with the income of another person is involved. Measuring the amount of poverty in an economy is also, however, a non-trivial exercise. Again, alternative formulas have been suggested. One of the simplest (and, therefore, the most widely used) formulas is the so-called *Head Count Ratio* which is the proportion of the population with incomes below the poverty line. It has, however, been pointed out that poverty also may have a relative aspect after all. How poor (i.e. how *deprived*) a person considers himself or herself to be may be an important consideration in deciding whether he or she is to be called poor. Now, the sense of deprivation that a person has may well depend not only on his or her own income but also on the incomes of others. In other words, it is possible that measuring poverty would also involve interpersonal comparisons. The notion of poverty that takes into consideration this aspect of the matter is called *relative poverty*. It is intuitively obvious, however, that relative poverty is notionally very close to inequality. Usually, when we talk about poverty in an economy, it is understood that what we have in mind is the absolute aspect of poverty.

References

Atkinson, A.B. (2015): *Inequality: What Can Be Done?*, Harvard University Press, Cambridge, MA.

Chancel, L., Piketty, T., Saez, E. and Zucman, G. (2022): *World Inequality Report 2022*, Bellknap Press, Cambridge, MA.

Dabla-Norris, E., Kochhar, K., Suphaphiphat, N., Ricka, F. and Tsounta, E. (2015): *Causes and Consequences of Income Inequality: A Global Perspective*, IMF Staff Discussion Note, June. International Monetary Fund, Washington, DC

Kundu, S. and Cabrera, M. (2022): "Fiscal policies and their impact on income distribution in India", Working Paper 120, April, CEQ Institute, Tulane University. The institute, Tulane.

Mahendra-Dev, S. (2018): "Inequality, employment and public policy", Working Paper 2018-003, January, Indira Gandhi Institute of Development Research, Mumbai.

Qureshi, Z. (2023): '*Rising inequality: A major issue of our time*', www.brookings.edu/article/rising-inequality-a-major-issue-of-our-time/last accessed on September 3, 2023.

WEF.(2013): *Outlook on the Global Agenda 2014*, World Economic Forum, Geneva.

World Bank.(2006): *World Development Report 2006*, World Bank, Washington DC. www.sdgs.un.org last accessed September 3, 2023.

2 Inequality
The salient facts

2.1 Introduction

Chapter 1 repeatedly referred to the issue of rising inequality without saying anything precise about how fast it is rising or how high the level of inequality is in today's world. The purpose of the present chapter is to apprise the reader of the salient facts and figures in these regards. Section 2.2 seeks to describe the global picture while Section 2.3 is devoted to the Indian scenario. Section 2.4 concludes this discussion.

2.2 The global scenario

2.2.1 Decreasing income inequality between countries in recent decades

Global income inequality, that is, inequality in the distribution of income among people of the world as a whole can be thought of as a combination of (1) inequality between countries and (2) inequality within countries. In this subsection, we concentrate on the first type of inequality. For this part, one possible approach is to consider each country as one unit and to define global inequality as the inequality between the *per capita* incomes of the countries. Thus, if there are n countries in the world with per capita incomes $y_1, y_2, \ldots, y_n$, then it is as if there are just n individuals in the world with the income of an individual taken to be equal to the per capita income of the country to which he or she belongs.

The very first problem that arises under this approach is that the per capita incomes of different countries are expressed in different monetary units. How do we make them comparable? An obvious way to do so, of course, would be to express the per capita incomes of the different countries in terms of some common currency such as the US dollar by using the official rate of exchange. This, however, does not solve the comparability problem completely. Frequently, it is the case that one US dollar will have different real purchasing powers in different countries. One US

DOI: 10.4324/9781032707082-2

dollar in the USA is not the same thing (in terms of real command over goods and services) as the Indian rupee equivalent of one US dollar in India at the official exchange rate. What is done to obtain comparability is to calculate the so-called *purchasing power parity* (PPP) exchange rate. For instance, to obtain the PPP exchange rate between the US dollar and the Indian rupee, we first construct a *commodity basket* composed of specified amounts of different commodities. We then compare the cost of this basket in the currencies of the two countries. If the given basket costs 10 dollars in the USA and 500 rupees in India, then the dollar–rupee PPP exchange rate is \$10 = Rs. 500, that is, \$1 = Rs. 50. The convention is to express the per capita incomes of all countries in terms of US dollars using the PPP exchange rates. Suppose that these are $x_1, x_2, ..., x_n$. We would say that the vector $(x_1, x_2, ..., x_n) = \mathbf{x}$ (say) is the income distribution.

There are various inequality indices, that is, formulas for calculating the degree of inequality in a given distribution of a variable. The most widely used index of inequality is the Gini coefficient (or "the Gini" for short). The value of the Gini coefficient for a distribution $\mathbf{x}$, denoted by the symbol $G(\mathbf{x})$, is sometimes expressed as a *proportion*, that is, a number that varies between 0 and 1. The Gini formula is such that if $\mathbf{x}$ is a perfectly equal income distribution, that is, if everybody has the same income, then $G(\mathbf{x})$ will be zero. The more unequal it is, the closer will $G(\mathbf{x})$ be to 1. Sometimes, however, the coefficient is expressed as a *percentage* (rather than a proportion). In that case, it lies between 0 and 100 and the closer it is to 100, the greater is the inequality of the distribution. There is no standard practice in this regard. We shall use the 0 to 100 scale. (See the Appendix to this chapter for a discussion of how the Gini coefficient is calculated).

The way of measuring inter-country income inequality outlined above, however, has an obvious defect. It ignores the fact that *population size* differs between countries. Since we are interested in inequality among the people of the world and there are more people in some countries than in others, it would be wrong to compare the per capita incomes of the countries on a one-to-one basis. Rather, each country's per capita income needs to be weighted (i.e. multiplied) by the *proportion* of the world population living in the country. Thus, if the proportion of people living in country 1 is w_1, that in country 2 is w_2 and so on, we should consider the *population-share-weighted* per capita (PPP dollar) incomes of the countries $(w_1 x_1, w_1 x_2, ..., w_n x_n) = \mathbf{z}$ (say) and apply the index formula on the vector $\mathbf{z}$ rather than on $\mathbf{x}$. If the Gini index formula is applied, what we get is called the population-share-weighted Gini coefficient of inter-country income inequality. For convenience, we shall call it the inter-country Gini.

Now, what can we say about the trend of inter-country inequality (as measured by the inter-country Gini) over time? Researchers do not seem to agree over all the fine details of the trend. For instance, Sutcliffe (2004), based on data compiled by Maddison (2003), reports that between 1950 and 1960, the inter-country Gini decreased from about 55 to about 54 but increased from 1960 to 1980 when it reached 57. Since 1980 till now, however, it has been declining. The figure for 2020 is about 54. Milanovic (2016), however, reports that while there have always been year-to-year fluctuations, there has been an overall falling trend in the Gini coefficient since about 1960 till 2010 although the pace at which it has fallen has quickened after 1980. As per UN (2013), the value of the coefficient fell from 63 in 1980 to 53 in 2012.

On the other hand, there is considerable agreement among researchers that inter-country inequality increased continuously for a long time since the beginning of the Industrial Revolution.

Thus, there is overall agreement that income inequality between countries increased over the major part of the nineteenth century as well as the early decades of the twentieth, but has started decreasing from 1980, if not earlier, although there are differences in the precise values of the Gini coefficient for the different years reported by different researchers.

The reason behind this observed overall time pattern is not far to seek. For a long time since the advent of the Industrial Revolution, the countries of the West enjoyed high rates of growth of per capita income while much of the rest of the world experienced negligible growth (if not actual decay). In fact, as is well-known, there are grounds for believing that this was due not only to the accelerated growth of output in the West made possible by the new industrial technology but also to the fact that most of the newly industrialised countries were colonial powers and were able to use their colonies both as sources of raw materials used in their industries and as outlets for selling the produced goods, often under exploitive pricing arrangements. This is what caused inter-country inequality to increase. After the Second World War, the colonial era gradually came to an end. In this phase, although the *disparity of the growth rate* between the developed countries on the one hand and the newly developing countries on the other gradually diminished, the growth rate of the developed economies still continued for some time to be higher than that of the rest of the world. Thus, the *disparity between the per capita incomes* in the developed and the underdeveloped parts of the world continued to increase or, at least, did not fall very significantly.

Since around 1980, however, there has been a drastic change in the picture. Growth rates of the developed countries started falling behind those of many of the developing ones. First, there was a surge in the growth rates of some of the East Asian countries in the 1970s. This was followed by a leap in the growth rate of China in the 1980s. Starting from the 1990s India, too, registered a significant spurt in the growth rate. More recently, the growth rates of a number of other developing economies (such as Bangladesh and Vietnam) have also picked up significantly. On the other hand, there has been considerable deceleration in the growth rates of the developed countries. Moreover, it is the developing countries that account for the major part of the world population. No wonder, the population-share-weighted Gini coefficient of inter-country inequality of per capita income has fallen significantly in the last half-century. One can, thus, conclude that as per the most widely used index of inequality (viz, the Gini), income inequality *between* countries has decreased since about 1980.

2.2.2 Increasing income inequality within countries

2.2.2.1 Studies based on the Gini index

Consider now the matter of income inequality *within* countries. From the viewpoint of availability of data, estimating income inequality within a country is much more problematic than estimating inequality between countries. For the latter, we only need to know the population shares and the per capita incomes of the countries. The data for these are *relatively* easily available, at least for the years for which population census and national income accounting data of the countries can be accessed. This is not to belittle the painstaking research that has to be done in order to arrive at the required figures (in PPP dollars) for all the years of the time series. To estimate inequality within a country, however, we need the reports of surveys of incomes of *individuals* (or *households*) in the country. In economies such as India, it is difficult to collect data on personal or household incomes and, therefore, consumption (or more, generally, expenditure) is often used as a proxy variable for income. In any case, it is only on the basis of economy-wide field surveys that the income (or expenditure) distribution of a country can be constructed. One difficulty faced in conducting such surveys is that, because of practical reasons, it is difficult to interview *every* individual (or household) in an economy, especially one with a large population. Therefore, it is a *sample* drawn from the population that is studied. How to ensure that the sample is a *representative* one (i.e. it will represent the whole population), however, is a non-trivial question. It is this type of real-life issues that motivated the development of the theory of *random sampling*. The history of such surveys, however, does not go very far back in time.[1]

UN (2020) reported that between 1990 and 2016, the Gini coefficient of within-country income (or expenditure) distributions increased in 49 out of the 119 countries for which data were available. It declined in 58 countries and remained more or less the same in the other 12. However, as the report emphasised, the fact that only 49 (i.e. less than half) of the 119 countries displayed an upward trend in the Gini coefficient should *not* be taken to mean that less than half of the total population of these 119 countries were in countries with rising inequality. The catch is that most of the countries with *large populations* were among the 49 that experienced rising Gini. In fact, these countries (which included both China and India) were home to more than 70 per cent of the total population of the 119 countries and also to the majority of the global population. Thus, over the past three decades, the majority of the people of the world faced the problem of increasing inequality in the countries of their residence.

As stated before, in some developing countries such as those in Africa and in some parts of Asia (including India), the household surveys collect data on *consumption* while in the advanced countries and in the countries of Latin America and also in other parts of Asia (including China), the data relate to *income*. For this reason, the values of the Gini coefficient are not comparable across countries in all cases.[2]

It may be noted, however, that, by studying the cases of countries for which there happens to be estimates of both consumption Gini and income Gini, researchers have shown that the *time trend* of inequality in any given country is usually the same irrespective of whether it is the distribution of consumption or that of income that one is talking about. In other words, consumption inequality and income inequality usually move in the same direction (see World Bank (2016)). Thus, if one's main interest is in the direction of change of inequality within a country (i.e. whether inequality within the country has a rising or a falling trend over time), then it does not matter too much whether the index of inequality is the consumption Gini or the income Gini.

2.2.2.2 Studies based on income shares

The discussion so far has concentrated on the Gini coefficient as the only index of inequality since it is the index that has so far been used for the purpose of studying the time trend of inequality at the global level. Any inequality index (whether it is the Gini coefficient or not), however, has the limitation that it is a *summary* measure of inequality and does not pay attention to matters of detail. In particular, it does not consider the question whether changes in inequality are caused by changes in the top, middle or bottom parts of the income distribution (i.e. by changes in the shares of the rich, the middle classes or the poor in the total income).[3] These are, however, important aspects of the dynamics of income inequality.

For this reason, economists also use the share of, say, the top (i.e. the richest) 1 per cent or 10 per cent of the population in the total personal income as measures of inequality of income distribution. *Ratios* such as that between the shares of, say, the top 10 per cent and the bottom 10 per cent are also used. (The ratio between the shares of the top 10 per cent and the bottom 40 per cent is known as the *Palma Ratio*.) Inequality measures of this type correspond to our intuitive notion of inequality as concentration of income in the hands of the rich and are now widely applied for estimating inequality within countries as well as global inequality.

One advantage of the indices of inequality based on the top and bottom income shares is that, unlike the Gini coefficient, they do not necessarily require information on the complete income distribution. Hence, in many cases, they can be calculated even in the absence of comprehensive income surveys. Moreover, since, as noted before, income or consumption surveys began only in the later decades of the twentieth century, the time series of the Gini coefficient within a country often does not go very far back in time. Using the income-share-based indices, economists have been able to study the pattern of change in inequality within countries over a much longer span of time.

Inequality researchers now have access to a new source of data, *the World Inequality Database* (WID), that has been built up in the course of the past few decades. For a large number of countries, the WID reports the values of the Gini coefficient as well as income-share-based inequality measures calculated by integrating information from diverse data sources such as income and consumption surveys, national accounts statistics, tax records etc.

The newly amassed data reveal that in many countries, income has been increasingly concentrated in the hands of the rich over the recent few decades. Between 1990 and 2015, the share of total income going to the richest 1 per cent of the population increased in 59 out of the 100 countries for which data were available (UN (2020)). In 18 of these 59 countries, the richest 1 per cent earned more than 20 per cent of the total incomes in 2015. It is particularly noteworthy that these countries included some in which the Gini coefficient has *decreased* quite rapidly, confirming the suspicion that the Gini coefficient does not always show enough sensitivity to what is happening at the two ends, the top and the bottom, of the income distribution and needs to be supplemented by income-share-based measures of inequality (see Note 3). One striking example is that of Brazil where the share of the top 1 per cent increased from 26.2 per cent in 2001 to 28.3 per cent in 2015. The Gini coefficient, however, fell from 60 in 1995 to 53 in 2015.

Table 2.1, on the other hand, displays the patterns of change in the ratio between the shares of the top 10 per cent and bottom 50 per cent of the income distribution in selected years of the 200-year time span 1820–2020 in eight countries including some of the most populous countries of the world such as India, China, the USA and Brazil. As is seen from the table, the recent trends in inequality in all of the eight countries present a

Table 2.1 Inequality in selected countries and the world, 1860–2020. (Average income of top 10 per cent divided by average income of bottom 50 per cent)

	1820	1900	1950	1980	2020
World	18	40	40	52	37
Brazil	23	25	28	25	28
China	13	15	5	6	15
Great Britain	16	20	16	7	9
India	15	19	9	8	22
Japan	12	14	4	8	12
Russia	14	16	6	5	14
South Africa	19	23	23	18	56
USA	15	14	11	9	17

Source: Chancel and Piketty (2021, Table 7).

gloomy picture. The most striking case is that of South Africa where in 2020 the share of the top 10 per cent was as much as 56 times that of the bottom 50 per cent. In 1980, it was 18 times. In India, it was 8 times in 1980 but 22 times in 2020. Thus, as was the case (in subsection 2.2.2.1) with the analysis based on the Gini coefficient, the inescapable conclusion, again, is that the overwhelming majority of the world's population lives in countries that have experienced very sharp increases in inequality in the most recent decades, although in the preceding ones there had been fluctuation in the level of inequality in some of the countries.

The time pattern of changes in inequality in each of these countries remains roughly the same if we consider the ratio of the income shares of the top 1 per cent and the bottom 50 per cent of the income distributions. As expected, however, in any country, the degree of inequality in any given year in this case is greater than what it is in Table 2.1. We omit the details here (see Table 9 in Chancel and Piketty (2021)).

2.2.3 Increasing global inequality of income

Economists have also estimated the time trends of *overall* global inequality which is a combination of inequality between countries and inequality within the countries. Bourguignon and Morrison (2002) estimated the values of the Gini coefficient (and also those of a few other inequality indices such as the Theil index and the standard deviation of the logarithm of income) for the global income distribution for selected years in the time period 1820–1992. It was found that inequality increased from the beginning of the nineteenth century till the Second World War. After the war, it has stabilised or has increased slowly. These authors found that in the nineteenth century and in the first half of the twentieth century, most of the global inequality was due to inequality within

Table 2.2 Global Gini, 1820–1992, as per Bourguignon and Morrison (2002)

Year	1820	1850	1870	1890	1910	1929	1950	1960	1970	1980	1992
Gini	50.0	53.2	56.0	58.8	61.0	61.6	64.0	63.5	65.0	65.7	65.7

Source: Bourguignon and Morrison (2002).

countries. During 1950–1992, however, inequality between countries explained the major part (about three-fourths) of the global inequality. The values of the global Gini coefficient for the various years as estimated by these authors are shown in Table 2.2.

Lakner and Milanovic (2016) and Milanovic (2016) extended the Bourguignon–Morrison time series of global Gini up to 2010. They found very similar trends for the years up to about 1980. After that, however, the Gini coefficient was found to have declined a little. Moreover, inequality *between* (rather than within) countries was again found to be the main contributor to overall inequality in any given year in the recent decades. All of these authors also emphasised that although the global Gini has declined after 1980, it has remained at a quite high level. In 2010, it was about 70.0.

Estimates of the Gini coefficient, needless to say, are based on the data on income distributions collected through household income surveys. As we have said before, reliable survey data in this regard are available only from the 1950s onwards. At this point, therefore, the reader may ask how the Gini coefficients for the earlier years were calculated. Actually, these were based on ingenious and painstaking historical research that led to the unearthing of many indirect and fragmented evidences. These evidences were then woven into reasonable guesses about the income distributions on the basis of a series of plausible assumptions. Most economists find these guesses fairly acceptable.

Apart from the problem of the availability of comprehensive survey data for the nineteenth century and the early decades of the twentieth, however, there is another issue here. It has been observed that income surveys typically *underreport* top incomes. At the upper end of the income scale, there is a serious problem of concealment of incomes. As a result, income surveys typically understate the degree of inequality in the distribution of income. Moreover, since some incomes are underreported, it follows that total income and, therefore, the per capita income of the country are also underestimated by income surveys. In many cases, such underestimation can be directly verified. For instance, typically, the estimate of per capita income thrown up by income surveys do not tally with the per capita income obtained from the national income accounts. The former is significantly less than the latter. The problem has been known to researchers for quite some time (see Deaton (2005) and Ravallion (2003)). Moreover, recent research has found that the magnitude of the discrepancy between the estimates obtained from national accounts statistics and

Table 2.3 Global Gini, 1820–2021, as per the World Inequality Database

Year	1820	1910	1980	1990	2000	2010	2020	2021
Gini	60.0	72.0	69.0	70.0	71.0	68.0	67.0	67.0

Source: Chancel and Piketty (2021) and www.wid.world last accessed on September 13, 2023.

household income surveys is actually considerably larger than what it was previously thought to be (see Prydz et. al. (2022)).

In view of these facts, researchers have sought to improve on the estimates of the global Gini coefficients by using data from such sources as the WID referred to before (see Chancel and Piketty (2021)). In particular, the use of income tax and national accounts statistics data, in combination with income survey data, has led to what most economists believe to be better estimates of the Gini. Table 2.3 reports the global Gini coefficients for selected years estimated in this way. As expected, these estimates point towards the fact that inequality has often been somewhat higher than what was indicated by earlier estimates. Moreover, they show that the upward trend of global inequality continued till about the end of the twentieth century rather than till 1980. It is only after 2000 that the global Gini has declined a little.

The time trends of global income inequality measured by income shares (rather than by the Gini) are broadly similar though not exactly the same. Again, there were sharp increases throughout the nineteenth century and the first half of the twentieth century. The rate of increase moderated thereafter. The ratio of the top 10 per cent and the bottom 50 per cent income shares, however, does show a declining trend since 1980 although there was a slight increase from 31.58 per cent in 2020 to 32.24 per cent in 2021 (www.wid.world last accessed on September 12, 2023).

However, the main difference between the findings of Chancel and Piketty (2021) based on the WID on the one hand and those of Bourguignon and Morrison (2002) and Lakner and Milanovic (2016) on the other relate to the relative importance of the two components of overall global inequality viz. inequality between countries and inequality within countries. As stated before, the latter authors are of the opinion that ever since about 1950, inequality *between* countries has been the main contributor towards overall global inequality. In contrast, Chancel and Piketty (2021) find that while that may have been true for the second half of the twentieth century, more recently it is inequality *within* countries that has become the major contributor. If the ratio between the income shares of the top 10 per cent and the bottom 50 per cent is taken to be the measure of inequality, the switchover of the relative importance of the two contributing factors is seen to have taken place soon after 2000.

It needs to be emphasised that the question of relative importance of the two components of overall global inequality is not merely a matter of academic interest. It is a vital issue from the viewpoint of formulation of policies aimed at reducing inequality. If global inequality is mainly a matter of disparity between the per capita incomes of the countries, then the efforts to reduce inequality must be directed mainly at removing this disparity. Equality will prevail only if per capita incomes of the countries converge. In this case, policies must be mainly concerned with the development of the less-developed parts of the world. *Within* a less-developed country, how to increase GDP would then be the question of overriding importance. The task of reducing inequality within the country would then take a back seat. On the other hand, if inequality within countries is the main driver of global inequality, then, obviously, the war against inequality must be fought at the country level. Each country would need to reduce inequality within its boundary. The finding by Chancel and Piketty (2021) mentioned in the previous paragraph, therefore, implies that in today's world, it is the need for country-level actions to reduce inequality that demands the major share of our attention.[4]

2.2.4 Global trends in wealth inequality

2.2.4.1 Trend of the wealth Gini

So far the focus of the discussion has been on income inequality. It needs to be noted, however, that the standard of living of an individual depends not only on the individual's income but also on his or her wealth. This is particularly true in the less-developed economies where the majority of the population does not have social security coverage. As a result, many people do not have any resources (other than their personal wealth) to fall back upon in case of an income disruption (such as a health emergency or a natural calamity). Inequality of living standards is, therefore, determined to a significant extent by inequality of wealth as well. This subsection is devoted to a brief discussion of the trends of wealth inequality.

The wealth of an individual is measured by his or her net worth (i.e. assets minus liabilities). One reason why our discussion of wealth inequality would be brief is that the collection of data on personal assets and liabilities is even more problematic than the collection of income or consumption data. Again, this is especially the case in less-developed economies. For this reason, inequality indices (such as the Gini coefficient) that require knowledge about the whole distribution of the variable are particularly difficult to calculate when the variable is wealth rather than income or consumption. Nevertheless, with improvements in methods of data collection and processing, some estimates of the wealth Gini in the recent decades are now available.

Commonsense tells us that wealth inequality is likely to be more severe than income inequality because a person's present wealth is, to a large extent, determined by his or her past incomes over a period of time. Hence, the accumulated effect of income inequality in all of the past years is likely to be reflected in the magnitude of wealth inequality that prevails at present. This intuitive notion is corroborated by the available estimates of the wealth Gini. It is seen that the Gini coefficients of the wealth distributions are usually by far larger than those of income distributions. So far as the *global* wealth distribution is concerned, Credit Suisse (2022) reports that the estimated Gini coefficient was as high as 91.9 in 2000, 89.4 in 2008 and 88.9 in 2021. There has, thus, been a slight downward trend in the global wealth Gini in the first two decades of the twenty-first century. The high *level* of the coefficient even in the most recent years, however, remains a cause for worry.

As is the case with income inequality, wealth inequality also can be considered to be determined by inequality between countries and inequality within them. In the case of wealth, however, it is the between-countries inequality that has always been seen to play the dominant part. Since, broadly speaking, wealth accumulation in a country goes hand-in-hand with its economic growth, the slight downward trend in the wealth Gini in the most recent decades is usually ascribed to the facts that over the recent decades the advanced economies of the West have been growing at a much slower pace than the emerging economies in the other parts of the world and that, therefore, between-countries wealth inequality has tended to decrease a little.

However, there is no denying the fact that inequality *within* countries has also always remained high. The values of the wealth Gini coefficient in some of the advanced and emerging economies for a number of years are displayed in Table 2.4. As is seen from the table, each of these countries displayed a high level of wealth inequality throughout the first two

Table 2.4 Wealth Gini in selected countries, 2000–2021

	2000	2005	2010	2015	2020	2021
Brazil	84.5	82.7	82.1	88.7	88.9	89.2
China	59.5	63.8	70.0	71.2	70.5	70.1
India	74.6	80.9	82.1	83.3	82.3	82.3
Japan	64.5	63.1	62.5	63.6	64.4	64.7
Russia	84.8	87.1	90.0	89.5	87.7	88.0
UK	70.5	67.6	69.1	73.0	71.7	70.6
USA	80.6	81.1	84.1	84.9	85.0	85.0

Source: Credit Suisse (2022).

Table 2.5 Wealth share of top 1 per cent in selected countries, 2000–2020

	2000	2010	2020
Brazil	44.2	40.2	49.5
China	20.7	31.5	30.8
India	33.2	41.4	40.5
Japan	20.4	16.7	18.1
Russia	54.4	62.8	58.1
UK	22.1	23.6	23.1
USA	32.9	33.4	35.3

Source: Credit Suisse (2022).

decades of the present century. Brazil, Russia and the USA are among the countries where the wealth Gini has been very high in all of these years. It has been relatively low in Japan. China which was the least unequal of these countries in 2000 lost this position to Japan in the later years.

2.2.4.2 Trend of wealth shares

The pattern of wealth inequality has also been studied in terms of the share of the rich in the total wealth. The findings are broadly similar to those based on the Gini coefficient. For instance, Credit Suisse (2022) reports that the richest 1 per cent people in the world owned 48.2 per cent, 42.7 per cent and 45.6 per cent of global wealth in 2000, 2008 and 2021, respectively. So far as the share of the richest 10 per cent was concerned, the figures for these three years were 88.8 per cent, 84.3 per cent and 81.9 per cent, respectively.

Not much is known about the long-run time trend of global wealth inequality measured by wealth shares. However, Alvaredo et. al. (2018) state that between 1980 and 2018 the top 1 per cent share in the total wealth in the advanced countries and China increased from 28 per cent to 33 per cent while the share of the bottom 70 per cent hovered around 10 per cent.

A little more, however, is known about the state of affairs *within* some countries in recent times. Table 2.5 shows the richest 1 per cent's wealth shares in some recent years in selected countries.

2.3 The Indian scenario

2.3.1 Trend of consumption inequality

This section takes a look at the trend of inequality in India. As mentioned before, in view of the difficulties of collecting data on household incomes, in India (as well as in some of the other countries) the official agencies that conduct household surveys often take consumption expenditure as the proxy for income. Although the distribution of consumption does not reveal the full picture of the income distribution, it is of interest not only as a proxy but also as an indication of the distribution of well-being in the economy. In this subsection, we summarise the available information on the trend of consumption inequality in India since the early 1980s.

The standard source of data on consumption expenditure in India is the five-yearly large-sample surveys conducted by the National Statistical Office (NSO), previously known as the National Sample Survey Office (NSSO) and as the National Sample Survey Organisation before that. The years for which the official reports on the distribution of consumer expenditure are available since the 1980s are 1983, 1987–88, 1993–94, 1999–2000, 2004–05 and 2011–12.[5] The next survey was scheduled for 2016–17 but was delayed by a year. However, at the time of writing this book (September 2023), the report on the 2017–18 survey is still not officially available.

Even among the inequality estimates for the years for which the survey reports are available, there is a problem of comparability. When the surveys are carried out, the households (or their heads) are asked to recall their expenditure on various items over a specified period (for instance, one month) prior to the date of the interview. This is called the *recall period*. In the surveys of 1983, 1987–88 and 1993–94, the NSSO used a uniform recall period (URP) of 30 days.

In most of the other countries, however, the practice is to use a mixed recall period (MRP) with a shorter recall period for high-frequency items (such as food items) and a longer one for low-frequency items (such as durable consumer goods). In an attempt to bring the Indian surveys in line with the global practice, MRP was used in 1999–2000. Economists pointed out that while there was nothing wrong with this, the estimates of inequality (and also of *average* consumption) obtained in this way are not comparable with those of the earlier surveys (see Deaton (2003)). Since comparability across years is important for finding the time trend of inequality, the years 1999–2000 will be dropped from the time series in the discussion below.

The 2004–05 survey found a way of using MRP and permitting comparability with the 1983, 1987–88 and 1993–94 surveys at the same time. A 30-day URP was used for collecting information on *all* items of expenditure. Additionally, however, a recall period of 365 days was used for such items as clothing, bedding, footwear, institutional medical care, education and consumer durables. Both sets of data were reported. Researchers, therefore, were able to use the part of the data that was based on URP for obtaining inequality estimates that are comparable with those of 1983, 1987–88 and 1993–94. A similar procedure can be applied to the 2011–12 survey data although that survey produced an even richer variety of data based on different types of commodity classifications and different recall periods. For a more detailed discussion of these comparability issues see, for instance, Banerjee (2020, 111–113).

Based on the 30-day URP, the Gini coefficients of the distribution of *monthly per capita consumer expenditure* (MPCE) of households (i.e. monthly household expenditure divided by household size) for the five years 1983, 1987–88, 1993–94, 2004–05 and 2011–12 have been reported to be 32.1, 32.6, 31.7, 34.4 and 35.7 (www.data.worldbank.org last accessed on September 14, 2023). Inequality (as per this inequality index) is, therefore, seen to have declined in India in the later part of the 1980s and increased thereafter.[6]

The latest official estimate of consumption Gini (35.7 in 2011–12) in India may not seem to be very high by international standards. The catch, of course, is that most of the other countries report the income Gini. As we have remarked before, the consumption Gini is an underestimate of the income Gini. If the correction factor discussed in Note 2 is applied on the consumption Gini, the income Gini in India in 2011–12 would be estimated to be 60.69 and that would place India among the countries with the highest income Ginis. A correction factor of 0.6 (which is recommended by some authors on the basis of the Gini estimates of *all* countries for which both consumption Gini and income Gini are available) will yield the value 57.12 which will also place India among the relatively high-inequality countries. Among the least unequal economies of the world (as per the criterion of the Gini coefficient) are the Scandinavian countries where the income Gini is typically less than 30. Many other western economies and Japan also have low Gini values, typically less than 40. More tellingly, some of India's neighbouring countries (including Bangladesh) which follow the practice of reporting the consumption Gini posted lower values of the coefficient in 2011–12.

2.3.2 Trend of income inequality

As stated before, the WID which makes use of income tax data contains estimates of the inequality of the *income* distributions of countries for which such data are available. Table 2.6 displays both the Gini coefficients and the ratio of the shares of the richest 10 per cent and the poorest 50 per cent of the population in the total personal income of the country for a number of selected years in the time span 1951–2014. As is seen from the table, both the Gini coefficient and the T10/B50 ratio indicate that income inequality in India fell steadily between 1965 and 1981 and has risen steadily since then. As expected, the magnitude of income inequality is greater than that of consumption inequality. The figures for the income

Table 2.6 Inequality of income distribution in India, selected years, 1951–2014. World Inequality Database

Year	'51	'65	'61	'71	'81	'90	'95	2000	'05	'10	'14
Gini	49.0	51.0	49.0	46.0	43.0	0.46	50.0	51.0	56.0	61.0	63.0
T10/ B50	9.88	11.33	9.87	8.60	7.37	8.48	10.39	11.03	14.12	18.57	21.76

Source: www.wid.world last accessed on September 16, 2023.

Note: T10/B50 = Ratio of the shares of the top 10 per cent and the bottom 50 per cent of the income distribution.

Gini coefficient confirm the suspicion (expressed above in the context of the consumption Gini) that by the early 2010s, the Indian economy had become one of the most unequal economies in the world. (Brazil and South Africa are among the few countries that have even higher Gini). Again, as in the case of the consumption Gini, the income Gini in India in 2014 shown in the table is greater than that in some of her neighbours (not shown in the table). For instance, it was about 54.0 in 2014 in Bangladesh.

In connection with the estimation of income inequality in India mention should also be made of the Indian Human Development Surveys (IHDSs) conducted by the National Council of Applied Economic Research (NCAER) in collaboration with the University of Maryland in 2004–05 and 2011–12. A third survey is reported to be underway at the time of writing this book. The IHDSs collect data on a variety of social and economic variables including income. A strong point of these surveys is that these are among the rare instances of attempts to collect *panel data* on the well-being of households in India. Under the panel approach, a random sample of households is drawn and these *same* households are then interviewed in the surveys of the different years. The procedure obviously gives a good idea about how the households' incomes (and other attributes) are evolving over time. The IHDSs reported that there was virtually no change in the Gini coefficient of the income distribution between 2004–05 and 2011–12. In both years, it was about 54.0. (The consumption Gini, however, increased and, as expected, in both years it was less than the income Gini.) See Desai et. al. (2010) for the results on the 2004–05 survey and Desai and Vanneman (2018) for those of 2011–12. Unfortunately, as pointed out by critics, the IHDSs are beset with a number of methodological issues so far as the income data are concerned. See, for instance, Bakshi et. al. (2012). Besides, what we are primarily interested here is the *trend* of inequality over time, and the inequality estimates for just the two years 2004–05 and 2011–12 are not of much help in this regard.

2.3.3 Trend of wealth inequality

As in the case of income (or consumption), the true picture of the distribution of wealth among households can only be obtained from primary surveys of the households. Unfortunately, household wealth survey data are even scantier than data from household income or consumption surveys. This subsection briefly reviews whatever little evidence regarding the trend of wealth inequality in India we have from primary surveys.

The principal source of primary data on the distribution of household wealth in India is the All India Debt and Investment Surveys (AIDISs) that are conducted every ten years or so. The precursors of the AIDISs were the All India Rural Credit Survey of the year 1950–51 and the All India Rural Debt and Investment Survey of 1961–62. Both of these surveys were conducted by the Reserve Bank of India (RBI). As the names of the surveys make clear, however, these were confined to the rural sector. It was in the AIDIS of the year 1971–72, conducted, again, by the RBI, that the scope of the survey was extended to the entire economy. For unknown reasons, however, the results of this survey were never made public. It was from 1981–82 that RBI entrusted the NSSO with the work of carrying out the AIDISs. The 1981–82 survey report is available. However, the information in the published report does not seem to suffice for the purpose of estimating the all India wealth distribution.

The reports of the 48th, 59th and 70th Rounds of AIDIS published in 1992, 2003 and 2013 do contain the information necessary for estimating the distributions of household *assets* in India in 1991, 2002 and 2012, respectively. It also contains information on the *average values* of household *net worth* in India (defined by NSSO to mean assets minus *loans repayable*) in these three years. However, the *distributions* of net worth among the households are not easily obtained from these reports. (This is especially true of the year 1991).

Under these circumstances all that is definitely known about the trend of household wealth distribution on the basis of actual household surveys is the trend of the *assets* distribution and that too only over the period between 1991 and 2012. Calculations done by the present author on the basis of the AIDIS data reveal that the household asset distribution in India was more unequal in 2012 than that in 1991 or 2002.[7] For instance, between 1991 and 2012, the shares of the bottom 20, 40, 60 and 80 per cent of the population in terms of asset ownership in 1991 were 1.01 per cent, 5.26 per cent, 14.25 per cent and 31.91 per cent, respectively. In 2012, these shares fell to 0.73 per cent, 3.59 per cent, 9.68 per cent and 23.03 per cent, respectively. On the other hand, the share of the wealthiest 20 per cent rose from an already very high figure of 68.09 per cent in 1991 to an even higher figure of 76.97 per cent in 2012. A comparison of the asset distribution in 2002 and 2012 reveals a similar rise in asset inequality in India between these two years.

Since asset distribution is only a partial description of the distribution of wealth, it is important to look at the attempts that have been made to estimate the inequality of wealth in India by considering both the assets and liabilities sides of the picture. Credit Suisse (2022) has sought to combine the AIDIS data with what is called the *household balance sheets* (HBSs). Ideally, the national accounts statistics of a country for every year should include a balance sheet (i.e. a statement of the stocks of assets and liabilities) for each sector of the economy at the end of the year. Unfortunately, India does not have an official balance sheet for the household sector for any year. Some academic researchers have attempted to fill the gap. Malhotra and Chandra (2019) constructed a HBS for *financial* assets and liabilities in India for a number of years up to 2017–18. These HBS estimates, in conjunction with AIDIS data, have been used by Credit Suisse (2022) to estimate the inequality of household *wealth* (rather than only the asset) distributions in India in some selected years starting from 2000.

It should be noted, however, that Credit Suisse data relate to distribution of wealth *per adult* (rather than per capita) in the household. In other words, the wealth distribution that is considered here is the distribution of wealth among the adults in the country rather than among the whole population. Theoretically, there are arguments both for and against using the household wealth data in this form. If the focus is on the well-being of the household (i.e. on the well-being of *all* members of the family), then it is household wealth per capita that is important. This has been the Indian tradition. However, if wealth is taken to be a measure of economic power, then there are grounds for focusing on wealth per adult in the family since children usually have little formal or actual wealth ownership. Moreover, since the use of household wealth per adult in this context is an international practice, converting the Indian data to this form is useful for the purpose of international comparisons.

Be that as it may, we report here the Credit Suisse (2022) findings regarding the Gini coefficient as well as the wealthiest 1 per cent's share in total household wealth (of the adults) for a number of years. See Table 2.7. As per these estimates, the Gini coefficient increased monotonically

Table 2.7 Wealth inequality in India, selected years, 2000–2021. Estimates by Credit Suisse

Year	2000	2005	2010	2015	2020
Gini	74.6	80.9	82.1	83.3	82.3
Top 1% share	33.2	41.9	41.4	42.3	40.5

Source: Credit Suisse (2022, Table 5, 31).

Table 2.8 Inequality of net personal wealth in India, selected years, 1995–2021. World Inequality Database

Year	1995	2000	2005	2010	2015	2021
Gini	0.68	0.68	0.68	0.72	0.75	0.75
T10/B50	32.78	33.19	32.55	44.13	53.12	54.07

Source: www.wid.world last accessed on September 21, 2023.

Note: T10/B50 = Ratio of the shares of the top 10 per cent and bottom 20 per cent of people in the wealth distribution.

between 2000 and 2015 and then fell slightly. The top 1 per cent's share in wealth has had more fluctuations. Both the inequality indices, however, indicate that there was considerably greater wealth inequality in India in 2020 than in 2000. They also show that the biggest upward jump in inequality was registered between the years 2000 and 2005.

A time series of the wealth inequality indices in India are also available in the WID. The values of the Gini coefficient as well as the ratio between the wealth shares of the wealthiest 10 per cent and the least wealthy 50 per cent among the adults of the country for the time period 1995–2021 are shown in Table 2.8. A strong point of these estimates is that they were arrived at by supplementing the AIDIS data with information from a number of other sources such as tax data. For a long time since the 1950s, India had a wealth tax in place. It was, however, discontinued since 2016. Currently, the findings reported in Table 2.8 are considered by most economists to be the best available time series on wealth inequality in India.[8]

2.4 Conclusion

The purpose of this chapter has been to give the reader a view of the "wealth of data" on economic inequality that has been amassed by researchers over the past few decades. Since inequality is what this book is about, the time trends of economic inequality in India and in the world needed to be highlighted to provide a background for the discussions in the remaining chapters. To summarise, it is seen that both income and wealth inequalities have been rising in India (as also in a number of other developing economies) for several decades now. Globally also, wealth inequality has been increasing fast. While global income inequality (as distinguished from income inequality *within* the countries) has, for the moment, stabilised a little, it has stabilised at a very high level which is a cause for worry. Moreover, many experts (for instance, Chancel and Piketty (2021)) have expressed the apprehension that it, too, may rise in the future.

Appendix to Chapter 2: The Gini coefficient

Since the discussion in this chapter has referred frequently to the Gini coefficient as the measure of inequality, the reader may wish to know how this coefficient is calculated. The coefficient is named after Corrado Gini, the Italian statistician, who suggested this measure of inequality in 1912. It is now known that there are several alternative ways in which the definition of the Gini coefficient can be stated. For the present purposes, it would suffice to state and briefly discuss just one of them. The coefficient is stated here as a proportion, that is as a number lying between 0 and 1. If the 0 to 100 scale is desired, it is to be multiplied by 100.

It may be assumed, without loss of generality, that the variable under consideration is *income*. Exactly, the same formula would apply to any other economic variable such as consumption or wealth.

Suppose that there are n individuals. They are listed in any order (for instance, in the alphabetical order of their names). Let the vector $(x_1, x_2, ..., x_n) = \mathbf{x}$ (say) be the income distribution, that is, let x_1 be the income of the first individual on the list, x_2 that of the second individual and so on. Let $\mathbf{y} = (y_1, y_2, ..., y_n)$ be the vector obtained by *rearranging* the components of $\mathbf{x}$ in *non-increasing* order. For instance, if there are five individuals and if $\mathbf{x} = (20, 50, 30, 10, 15)$, then $\mathbf{y}$ would be $(50, 30, 20, 15, 10)$. Let μ denote the average income, that is, the arithmetic mean of the income distribution. In the example, since total income is 125, μ is $125/5 = 25$.

Now, let $G(\mathbf{x})$ denote the value of the Gini coefficient for the income distribution $\mathbf{x}$. One definition of the Gini says that, for any $\mathbf{x}$,

$$G(\mathbf{x}) = 1 + (1/n) - \left[2/(n^2\mu)\right](y_1 + 2y_2 + 3y_3 + ... + ny_n). \qquad (2.1)$$

In the example above, $G(\mathbf{x}) = 1 + (1/5) - [2/(5^2 \times 25)](50 + 2 \times 30 + 3 \times 20 + 4 \times 15 + 5 \times 10]$ which is seen to be $38/125 = 0.304$. In percentage terms, the Gini coefficient of the income distribution $\mathbf{x}$ is, therefore, $0.304 \times 100 = 30.4$.

If $\mathbf{x}$ is a perfectly equal income distribution, that is, if everybody gets the same income so that everybody's income is equal to the average income μ, Eqn. (2.1) would reduce to $G(\mathbf{x}) = 1 + (1/n) - [2/(n^2\mu)](\mu + 2\mu + 3\mu + ... + n\mu) = 1 + (1/n) - [2/n^2\mu]\mu(1 + 2 + 3 + ... + n)$. Using the fact that the sum of the first n natural numbers, $(1 + 2 + 3 + ... + n)$, is $n(n + 1)/2$, it is easily seen that $G(\mathbf{x})$ in this case is zero.

On the other hand, in the case of maximum inequality where the total income (which is $n\mu$) goes to just one person and everybody else gets zero income, Eqn. (2.1) would reduce to $G(\mathbf{x}) = 1 + (1/n) - [2/(n^2\mu)](n\mu + 0 + 0 + ... + 0) = 1 + (1/n) - [2/(n^2\mu)]n\mu = 1 + (1/n) - 2/n = (n - 1)/n$. As n increases, the last expression approaches 1. Thus, in a large economy (such as that of India), it is approximately 1. In percentage terms, it is approximately 100.

As mentioned above, there are a number of alternative forms of the definition of the Gini. All of them are, however, *equivalent* in the sense that, for any given distribution $\mathbf{x}$, $G(\mathbf{x})$ would be exactly the same, no matter which of these alternative formulas is used to calculate it.[9] For some of the other algebraic definitions of the Gini, see Sen (1997, 30–31). An advanced treatment is Yitzhaki and Schechtman (2013).

The reader is reminded that the Gini coefficient is not the only available index of inequality. There are many others. (Sen (1997, Chapter 2) contains a review). The Gini is, however, the measure of inequality that is most widely used.

Notes

1 It all began in the 1950s. Indian statisticians and economists played a pioneering role in the matter. The Indian Statistical Institute and the National Sample Survey Organisation, two organisations founded by Professor P. C. Mahalanobis, developed the basic methodology and also carried out the field surveys. Needless to say, the methodology has been vastly improved upon since the days of the early start and a large number of researchers from all over the world have contributed to the process. It may also be noted that expenditure surveys of *selected groups of people* (such as industrial workers) have a longer history. The first of this kind of survey was the expenditure survey conducted by the Bureau of Labor Statistics in the USA over the period 1888–91 for the purpose of studying the spending pattern of workers. It is clear that for the purpose of estimating the Gini coefficient of income or expenditure in an economy, we need surveys encompassing all sections of the population.

2 In particular, since in any country the rich save a greater (and consume a smaller) proportion of their incomes than the poor and the middle classes, the inequality of the distribution of consumption is typically less than that of the income distribution. In other words, countries that report consumption Gini tend to *underestimate* their true (i.e. income) inequality. For instance, in Egypt, the Gini coefficient for consumption was estimated by the World Bank to be 31.5 in 2011 while the Luxembourg Income study estimated the Gini coefficient for income in the same country to be 53.9 in 2012 (see UN (2020, 54)). This type of finding has led some researchers to attempt cross-country comparisons of the Gini coefficients by converting, if necessary, an estimate of a consumption Gini into one of an income Gini by applying a correction factor on the former. If the estimates for Egypt are taken to be a guide, the correction would involve multiplying the consumption Gini by $53.9/31.5 = 1.7$ approximately.

3 In applied work, it is often seen that the Gini is affected more by changes in the middle part than by those at the top or the bottom.

4 Chancel and Piketty are, however, careful to remind the reader that while global inequality is now driven more by inequality within countries than by inequality between them, this should not be taken to

imply that between-country inequality has now become totally irrelevant. On the contrary, it remains quite high in absolute terms. Hence, reducing this type of inequality will also bring *some* benefits in terms of reducing global inequality.

5 The 1983 survey is so called because it was carried out over the calendar year 1983. Each of the other surveys was conducted in the relevant fiscal year.

6 MRP-based estimates of the Gini coefficients are also available for recent rounds of MCPE surveys. These reveal a similar trend. For instance, according to one estimate, the coefficient increased from about 35 in 2004–05 to about 37 in 2011–12 (see Himanshu (2019, Table 2)).

7 There was an issue of comparability between the findings of the 1991 and the 2002 surveys with those of 2012. In 1991 and 2002, household assets included all financial and physical assets (including durable household goods). In 2012, however, durable household goods were dropped from the list of assets because, on the one hand, the valuation of *used* household durable goods was found to be a difficult exercise and, on the other, the purchase of *new* durable household goods was included in the MPCE surveys. Academic researchers have tackled the resulting problem of non-comparability of the three surveys by recalculating the asset figures of the first two surveys by leaving out household durables (see Anand and Thampi (2016)). The findings reported in the text are based on this procedure.

8 Both Credit Suisse and WID also correct for the well-known problem of underreporting of wealth, especially by the very wealthy. For this purpose, they use, for instance, the data on the number of billionaires and their wealth published by the *Forbes Magazine*.

9 There is also a geometric way of calculating the Gini coefficient. It is related to the so-called *Lorenz curve* of a distribution which is a particular representation of the distribution. It can be shown that the value of the Gini coefficient for a distribution $\mathbf{x}$ is equal to the area between the Lorenz curve of $\mathbf{x}$ and that of the perfectly equal redistribution of $\mathbf{x}$ (i.e. of the distribution in which everybody's income is $\mu(\mathbf{x})$). The advantage of the algebraic definitions such as Eqn. (2.1) in the text, however, is that they enable us to compute the Gini coefficient directly from the given data without drawing the Lorenz curve.

References

Alvaredo, F., Chancel, L., Piketty, T., Saez, E. and Zucman, G. (2018): *World Inequality Report 2018*, World Inequality Lab, Paris.

Anand, I. and Thampi, A. (2016): "Recent trends in wealth inequality in India", *Economic and Political Weekly*, Vol. 51, 59–67.

Bakshi, A., Ramachandran, V.K., Rawal, V. and Swaminathan, M. (2012): "Household income surveys in India: Lacunae and illustrations from village surveys", *Paper Presented at the 32nd General Conference of the*

International Association for Research in Income and Wealth, Boston. Available on www.iariw.org last accessed on September 13, 2022.

Banerjee, A.K. (2020): *Measuring Development: An Inequality Dominance Approach*, Springer, New Delhi.

Bourguignon, F. and Morrison, C. (2002): "Inequality among world citizens: 1820–1992", *American Economic Review*, Vol. 92, 727–744.

Chancel, L. and Piketty, T. (2021): "Global income inequality, 1820–2020: The persistence and mutation of extreme inequality", Working Paper No. 2021/19, World Inequality Lab, Paris School of Economics, Paris.

Credit Suisse. (2022): *Global Wealth Report 2022*, Credit Suisse Research Institute, Geneva.

Deaton, A. (2003): "Adjusted Indian poverty estimates for 1999–2000", *Economic and Political Weekly*, Vol. 38, 322–326.

Deaton, A. (2005): "Measuring poverty in a growing world (or measuring growth in a poor world)", *Review of Economics and Statistics*, Vol. 87, 1–19.

Desai, S., Dubey, A., Joshi, B.L., Shariff, A. and Vanneman, R. (2010): *Human Development in India: Challenges for a Society in Transition*, Oxford University Press, New Delhi.

Desai, S. and Vanneman, R. (2018): *Indian Human Development Survey-II*, Inter-University Consortium for political and Social Research, Ann Arbor, MI.

Himanshu (2019): "Inequality in India: A review of levels and trends", WIDER Working Paper No. 2019/42, The United Nations University World Institute for Development Economics Research (UNU-WIDER), Helsinki.

Lakner, C. and Milanovic, B. (2016): "Global income distribution: From the fall of the Berlin Wall to the Great Recession", *World Bank Economic Review*, Vol. 30, 203–232.

Maddison, A. (2003): *The World Economy: Historical Statistics*, OECD, Paris.

Malhotra, A. and Chandra, T. (2019): "Indian household balance sheet: Accounting issues and financial wealth accumulation". DOI: 10.31124/advance.8113076

Milanovic, B. (2016): *Global Inequality: A New Approach for the Age of Globalization*, Harvard University Press, Cambridge, MA.

Prydz, E.B., Jolliffe, D. and Serajuddin, U. (2022): "Disparities in assessments of living standards using national accounts and household surveys", *Review of Income and Wealth*, Vol. 68, S385–S420.

Ravallion, M. (2003): "Measuring aggregate welfare in developing countries: How well do national accounts and surveys agree?", *Review of Economics and Statistics*, Vol. 85, 645–652.

Sen, A. (1997): *On Economic Inequality*, Oxford University Press, Oxford.

Sutcliffe, B. (2004): "World inequality and globalization", *Oxford Review of Economic Policy*, Vol. 20, 15–37.

UN. (2013): *Inequality Matters: Report on the World Social Situation 2013*, Sales No. 13.IV.2, United Nations, New York.

UN (2020): *World Social Report 2020: Inequality in a Rapidly Changing World*, Department of Economic and Social Affairs, United Nations, New York.

World Bank. (2016): *Poverty and Shared Prosperity 2016: Taking on Inequality*, World Bank, Washington D.C.

Yitzhaki, S. and Schechtman E. (2013): *The Gini Methodology*, Springer, New York.

3 Inequality and sluggish economic growth

A vicious circle

3.1 Introduction

In this chapter, we investigate the relation between inequality and economic growth. The purpose of the exercise is to establish the fact that the reasons for our concern for the problem of inequality extend beyond ethical or moral considerations. We distinguish between supply-constrained and demand-constrained economies. Section 3.2 considers a supply-constrained economy and shows that in such an economy, an increase in income and wealth inequality would reduce the rate of economic growth, especially in the long run and especially if the economy in question is a less-developed one. The matter has been the subject of some debate among economists, and from our viewpoint in this book, it is important to clarify what we can say on the matter with a reasonable degree of confidence. The section then proceeds to note that the relation between inequality and economic growth is not a one-directional one. The causation also runs in the other direction. Sluggish economic growth tends to increase income and wealth inequality. There is, thus, a vicious circle. High inequality slows down the growth rate and sluggish growth, in turn, increases inequality. Section 3.3 shows that largely the same statements apply for a demand-constrained economy. Section 3.4 concludes the chapter.

3.2 Inequality and economic growth in a supply-constrained economy

3.2.1 Supply-constrained and demand-constrained economies

Start by recalling that we are particularly interested in an economy such as that of India where per capita income or output is relatively low. From a commonsense viewpoint, if the actual level of output per capita is low, the reason must be that either the producers, for some reason, are unable to produce commodities in sufficient quantities or there is a problem of

DOI: 10.4324/9781032707082-3

demand deficiency (although there is adequate productive capacity). In the former case, the economy is said to be *supply-constrained*; in the latter case, it is said to be *demand-constrained*. This section is concerned exclusively with the case of the supply-constrained economy.

3.2.2 The importance of investment

Investment, it is said, is the prime mover of economic growth. The reason for this is easily appreciated in a supply-constrained economy. Economic growth is conventionally defined to mean the growth of per capita output in the economy. Since output per capita is the total output divided by the population size, the growth rate of output per capita is essentially the growth rate of output *minus* the growth rate of population. We shall, however, mostly talk about the growth of *output* itself (rather than of output per capita). So far as *short-run growth* (i.e. growth in the near future) is concerned, this would hardly make any difference since the population growth rate in a country can be taken to be fixed in the short run so that increasing the growth rate of output is necessary and sufficient for increasing the growth rate of output per capita. In the long run, however, the population growth rate is variable. Theoretically, therefore, it is possible to increase the growth rate of output per capita by reducing the population growth rate even if the growth rate of total output remains the same. In practice, however, not much can be achieved in this way within a reasonable time frame since the process of reducing the growth rate of population is time-consuming. Moreover, in many of the developing economies (including India), the population growth rate is now less than 2 per cent per annum (see United Nations (2022)). In these countries, therefore, the annual growth rate of output per capita cannot be increased in this way by more than 2 percentage points even if the growth rate of population is reduced to zero. In the advanced economies, the population growth rate is already nearly zero (or even negative). China is fast approaching this state. Thus, for all practical purposes, both in the short run and the long, the task of increasing the rate of growth of output (or income) per capita requires increasing the growth rate of (total) output.

Now, from the point of view of the economy as a whole, the amount of output that can be produced is limited by the amounts of the factors of production (mainly, land, labour and capital) that are available in the economy.[1] Land, however, is essentially fixed in supply. Productivity per unit (say, per hectare) of land may, of course, be sought to be increased (by such means as increasing irrigation facilities). But that requires *investment*. Again, labour supply is not a binding constraint for a less-developed economy where population is increasing and certainly for a country that already has a large population and finds it difficult to provide gainful employment to all who seek it. The supply of *skilled* labour is frequently in short supply in less-developed economies. However, transforming unskilled labour into skilled labour involves *investment* in human capital. Moreover, it often involves some investment in physical capital also. For instance, expanding health and educational facilities often requires investment in buildings and equipment. Thus, the effective constraint on growth in a supply-constrained economy is the limited amount of capital (defined to include both physical and human capital). This is what makes *investment* (defined to mean addition to the capital stock) the prime mover of economic growth.

3.2.3 *Effect of inequality on economic growth*

This subsection focuses on the effect of inequality on growth. There are a number of theories that establish that the effect of inequality on growth is *negative*. Three of the most important theories that explain how this negative effect arises are those relating to (1) credit market imperfections, (2) socio-political instability and (3) differential fertility. Some of the other approaches to the matter (such as what has been called the "political economy approach") and a *dissenting view* that considers the effect of inequality on growth to be positive (rather than negative) will also be discussed. This theoretical discussion will be followed by a look at what empirical observations tell us about the matter.

3.2.3.1 *Credit market imperfections*

In an ideal world where credit markets would work perfectly, investment decision of an investor would have nothing to do with his or her personal income or wealth. If a person has a good investment opportunity, it would not matter whether she has the resources to invest. She can always borrow. In fact, if the credit market is perfect, there would be a *single* interest rate at which anyone can borrow or lend any amount of money. Moreover, two persons with the same prospective return on an investment would invest the *same* amount, no matter whether or how much they differ in respect of the levels of their income or wealth. It is obvious that under these circumstances, the *rate of investment* in the economy, that is, the proportion of the total output that the people of the country decide to invest (rather than consume) would be independent of the income and wealth distributions in the economy. Therefore, so would be the growth rate of the economy.

The reality, however, hardly fits this description, especially if the economy in question is a less-developed one. One of the important ways in which it diverges from the model of a perfect credit market is that since borrowers may default on their loans, lenders typically demand *collateral assets* as securities. These would be forfeited in case of non-repayment of the loans. At once, the pattern of asset ownership and, therefore, that of wealth distribution in the economy become important. For the same reason, lenders typically also look at the *incomes* of the prospective borrowers so that income distribution in the economy also becomes important. Therefore, in less-developed economies, there are investment opportunities that remain unutilised because of credit availability problems faced by borrowers who are unable to provide collaterals. In the real world, therefore, the higher the inequality of the income and wealth distributions (i.e. the higher the degree to which income and wealth are concentrated in the hands of a few), the greater is the percentage of the population that is excluded from making investments even when there are profitable investment opportunities.

The above argument contains a bit of oversimplification. In many cases, some of those who are unable to provide collaterals are not literally excluded from the credit markets. They may take recourse to the *informal credit market* in which moneylenders typically operate without any official permit or sanctions for their business. In the rural sector, the borrowers in the informal market are typically small and middle farmers and artisans. In the urban sector, these are typically small traders. The informal moneylenders sometimes lend *without* demanding collaterals. However, this does not make much difference to the arguments in the previous paragraph. The fact is that the informal lenders charge enormously high interest rates. One reason for this is that, like all lenders, they worry about the possibility of repayment defaults. In the absence of collaterals what they do is to spend a lot of resources on making their own private arrangements for monitoring the borrowers. The costs of these arrangements *partly* explain the exorbitantly high interest rates charged by them. The other part of the explanation lies in the fact that, given their need for loans that is not catered to by the formal sector lenders who demand collaterals, the borrowers are forced to approach lenders who can monitor them privately. (In the rural sector, it is typically the sole moneylender in the immediate neighbourhood or one of the lenders in villages that are very close by). This gives the moneylenders monopolistic or oligopolistic powers which they use to extract supernormal profits that more than compensate for the costs of monitoring.

Needless to say, the exceedingly high interest rates prevent the informal sector borrowers from undertaking investment projects that would have been profitable, had they been able to access the formal credit market.[2]

A related aspect of the matter is that inherited wealth is an important part of one's personal wealth and, in the presence of credit market imperfections, becomes an important determinant of the ability to invest. Moreover, in these circumstances, an initial inequality of inherited wealth has the possibility of being self-perpetuating and having an adverse impact on the long-run growth rate of the economy. The effect is significantly large, especially if human capital formation is an important issue since investment in education that is necessary for the purpose is a long-run investment.

Altogether, therefore, there are grounds for hypothesising that, in the presence of credit market imperfections, inequality of wealth and income inhibits investment. Therefore, the higher the inequalities of wealth and income, the lower will be the rate of economic growth. The reader interested in more detailed discussions of the matter and mathematical derivations may see, for instance, Banerjee and Newman (1993), Galor and Zeira (1993) and Loury (1981).

3.2.3.2 Socio-political instability

A number of economists have emphasised that inequality in the distribution of income and wealth motivates the poor to engage in crimes, riots and illegal activities of various other types. This has direct as well as indirect adverse implications for economic growth. The time and resources spent by the criminals in the process of perpetrating the crimes as well as the physical and monetary losses suffered by the victims of the crimes *directly* impose an economic burden on the economy. The *indirect* effects operate through the disruption of production processes that is caused by such activities and that may affect many more people. In extreme cases, inequality leads to revolutions and causes widespread destruction of life and capital stock. No less important is the fact that social upheavals affect the stability of political and social institutions including the legal framework. Property rights come under threat. Under these circumstances, people are loath to make investments, especially long-term ones. This affects the growth rate of the economy. Alesina and Perotti (1996) and Benhabib and Rustichini (1996) were among the early contributions to this line of research. More recent discussions include Aisen and Veiga (2013) and Hadzi-Vascov et. al. (2021).

3.2.3.3 Differential fertility

There is an important line of research that argues that if one has to understand the relation between inequality and economic growth, it is necessary to take account of the *fertility differences* between the rich and the poor. Richer families usually have *fewer* children than poorer ones. Moreover, an *increase* in inequality of wealth and income leads to *larger* fertility differentials (see, for instance, Kremer and Chen (2002)).

Building on these ideas, De la Croix and Doepke (2003) provided a novel explanation of why and how inequality hinders economic growth.

These authors noted the importance of human capital formation in determining the growth rate of a modern economy. Now, it is the amount of investment in education in an economy *today* that determines the amount of human capital in the economy in the *future* and, therefore, its future growth rate. The authors laid stress on the fact that the matter of fertility difference between the rich and the poor families is closely linked to that of *educational* differences between their children. If the cost of educating a child is fixed (i.e. if it does not depend on the income of the parents), education of a child is *relatively* expensive for poor parents in the sense that they have to spend a relatively high proportion of their income for the purpose. They, therefore, abstain from sending their children to school and substitute quantity for quality, preferring to have more children and to send them out to the job market as early as possible in order to boost the family income. On the other hand, bringing up a child takes up a fixed amount of the parents' *time*. Therefore, begetting many children is relatively costly for parents who earn high incomes because the time spent on rearing children is time taken away from income-earning activities. They can, however, afford the *cost* of educating the children.

Now, suppose that we measure today's investment in education by a *weighted average* of education of today's children in different families with different income levels where the weights are determined by the income-specific fertility rates (i.e. the weight of a family with a certain level of income is determined by the fertility rate in families in that income category). If there are significant rich–poor fertility differences and if these differences increase with an increase in economic inequality, then it is obvious that, in a more unequal economy, more weight will be put on families with less-educated children. The economy-wide average of the level of education of today's children will be lower. So, therefore, would be the future human capital stock of the country. This will reduce the future growth rate of the economy. Thus, inequality at present has a negative impact on growth in the future. The predictions of the theory regarding the relationships involving the three variables, inequality, fertility and growth, were also seen to be empirically valid.

It needs to be remembered, however, that investment in education has a longer gestation lag than physical investment in most cases. Educating today's children will make its effect felt only when the children grow up. Thus, "future economic growth" here refers to growth after a time gap of a *generation*. The authors also stressed that in this theory it was the fertility differences between the rich and the poor that played the crucial role in deriving a negative relation between inequality and economic growth. This was verified by the fact that if fertility was assumed to be constant (rather than income-dependent), inequality (measured by the Gini coefficient of the income distribution) would have a negligible effect on economic growth.[3]

3.2.3.4 *Political economy approach: Application of the median voter theorem*

There have also been *other* attempts to derive the proposition that inequality harms economic growth. Not all of these other theories, however, have found wide acceptance. Nevertheless, for the sake of completeness, reference should be made here to a theory that was proposed in the 1990s and was widely discussed for some time. It has been called the "political economy approach" and it uses what is called the *median voter theorem*.

Consider an economy with *n* persons. Recall (from Chapter 2) the notion of an income distribution, that is, a vector $\mathbf{x} = (x_1, x_2, ..., x_n)$ which is simply a listing of the incomes of the *n* individuals in the economy. Assume, for simplicity, that the incomes have been arranged in increasing order, that is, x_1 is the lowest income, x_2 is the second lowest income and so on. *Mean income* is simply the arithmetic mean of the *n* income levels (i.e. total income divided by the number of persons *n*), that is, the per capita income of the economy. *Median income* is that income level for which at least half of the population (i.e. at least *n*/2 persons) will have income levels that are less than or equal to it and at least half of the population will have income levels greater than or equal to it. For instance, if there are 5 persons with incomes of 10, 11, 12, 13 and 29 rupees, then the mean income is 75/5 = 15 rupees. The median income is 12 rupees because three out of the five individuals (i.e. more than half of the population) have incomes less than or equal to 12 and, again, three of them have incomes greater than equal to it.[4] We have deliberately chosen an example of an income distribution which is unequal in the intuitive sense that there is a large proportion (4 out of 5) of low-income persons and a small proportion (1 out of 5) of high-income ones. In such income distributions, the median is less than the mean.[5]

Suppose now that a society is considering a proposal suggesting that the government redistribute income from the relatively rich to the relatively poor by taxing the rich and putting income in the hands of the poor through its expenditure programmes. Suppose that the decision whether to accept or reject the proposal is to be arrived at by *majority voting*. It is obvious that if the income distribution is unequal, the *median voter*, that is, the voter whose income is the median of the income distribution, will be relatively poor in the intuitive sense that his or her income is less than the per capita (i.e. the mean) income of the country. Therefore, the median voter will stand to gain from the proposed redistributive programme and will, therefore, vote for it.

Now comes the median voter theorem which says that, under these circumstances, whichever alternative, accept or reject, the median voter votes for will be the winner in the voting.[6] It follows that the economy in question will go for the tax-financed government expenditure programme.

Now, the resulting taxes and subsidies will interfere with the process of resource allocation in the economy as determined by the free operation of the market forces. It is argued that this will interfere with the *efficiency* of resource allocation in the economy and that this, in turn, will reduce the growth rate of the economy. For instance, the taxes imposed on the richer sections of the population will reduce their work incentive and their propensity to invest. Thus, an unequal economy is likely to grow at a slow rate. Moreover, the higher the degree of inequality, the greater will be the magnitude of the proposed redistributive transfers from the rich to the poor and the stronger will be the forces that reduce investment and growth in the economy. Therefore, the effect of inequality on growth is negative.

While the theory is elegant, it has faced criticism regarding its empirical validity. As is easily seen, the result is derived from two distinct propositions (1) higher inequality leads to larger redistributive programmes and (2) the higher taxes on the rich required for financing the programmes reduce the growth rate of the economy. The first of these two propositions has been found to be empirically valid. See Milanovic (2000). (Some economists, however, have reported that there is not enough evidence to show that a more unequal economy necessarily imposes higher taxes on the rich). The second proposition does not perform well in empirical tests. It is not always the case that high taxes reduce the rate of economic growth. It all depends on the effect that government expenditure (financed by the taxes) has on productivity and investment in the economy. It is possible that government expenditure on physical and social infrastructure gives a sufficiently strong boost to productivity so that the growth rate actually increases. For further discussion on the political economy approach, see Alesina and Rodrik (1994), Bertola (1993), Perotti (1993) and Persson and Tabellini (1994).

3.2.3.5 Dissenting view: Positive effect of inequality on economic growth

While we are on the subject of the relation between inequality and economic growth, it should also be mentioned that there is a view that an increase in inequality would actually *increase* the growth rate. The argument that is usually advanced in support of this view is that richer individuals have higher *propensities to save* (i.e. that they save higher proportions of their incomes) than poorer ones. (The idea is based on the Keynesian view that poorer individuals, out of sheer necessity, spend a higher proportion of their income on *consumption* than richer ones. In other words, the poor has the higher *propensity to consume*. See Keynes (1920)). Hence, whenever there is a transfer of income from a poorer individual to a richer one (i.e. whenever inequality of income increases), the total savings in the economy will increase even though the total income remains the same. Therefore, the *saving rate* of the economy (i.e. the proportion of total income that the economy saves) will increase. Now, in a supply-constrained economy, the saving rate, it is argued, is the most important determinant of the growth rate because it is the saving rate that determines the rate of investment which is the prime mover of growth. See, for instance, Bourguignon (1981), Kaldor (1955) and Lewis (1954).

On close examination, however, the argument is seen to be flawed. For one thing, if the economy in question is an open one (i.e. if it engages in international trade), then *domestic* saving is not necessarily the only means of financing investment because there can be inflows of foreign capital. More important is the fact that, even in a closed economy, saving may not be the most important constraint on investment. Rarely does an investor use only his or her accumulated personal savings to finance a new investment project. Credit is the main source of funding for the purpose. Thus, while investment is certainly the prime mover of growth, the prime mover of investment is the supply of *credit* rather than that of savings as such. Hence, in a developing economy such as that of India, the kind of credit constraints that we have already discussed above is at least as important as (if not more so than) the problem of paucity of domestic saving.

It is also sometimes said that inequality promotes work effort because it induces people with low incomes to work harder in order to earn more. Inequality, therefore, is beneficial from the point of view of growth of output in the economy. Most development economists, however, do not take this argument seriously. While it is true that the poor are usually seen to work harder than the rich, it is more out of the sheer necessity to make ends meet than out of the desire to become rich someday. Moreover, in a populous country such as India, total output is unlikely to be constrained by the supply of total work effort. It is the crucial factor of production, capital, that is, in short supply. Investment, rather than the supply of physical effort, is the crux of the matter so far as economic growth is concerned.

3.2.3.6 What do the data say?

The discussion so far has been about *theories* relating to the effect of inequality on economic growth. What do actual data say about the sign of the effect? Is the empirically observed effect positive, negative or zero?

Since we are interested in the effect of inequality in a country on the country's growth rate, ideally we should undertake a *time series* study where data would be collected on a given country's rate of growth and its level of inequality *over time* (for instance, for a series of years). We would then check whether it is the case that the growth rate of the country has plummeted whenever inequality has increased and has shot up whenever inequality has decreased. We must, however, have a sufficiently long time series if we are to obtain good-quality estimates of the effect of inequality. Moreover, such a study would need to be carried out for each of a sufficiently large number of countries in order to ensure that our conclusion regarding the sign of the effect is generally valid rather than being true for only this or that specific country. Unfortunately, however, as we have seen in Chapter 2, it is for very few countries of the world that we have dependable estimates of inequality (such as those based on income or expenditure surveys) over sufficiently long periods of time. It is this paucity of data that has prevented researchers from taking this approach.

A more practical procedure would be to undertake *cross-section* studies. Here the idea is to fix a year and collect data on inequality levels and growth rates *for a number of countries* for the given year. We would then check whether countries with higher inequalities are the ones with lower rates of growth. If that is the case, then the effect is negative. Again, to ensure that the estimate of the effect is of good statistical quality, we need to have a sufficiently large number of countries in the sample. That, however, is not a problem if a relatively recent year is chosen. For such a year, data on the levels of inequality would be relatively easily available. (In practice, it is often not possible to find a specific year for which inequality measures are available for all the countries in the sample because the years in which the income surveys are carried out vary between countries. Effort, however, is made to ensure that the years of reference for the different countries are more or less adjacent).

Because of its practical feasibility, it was the cross-section approach that was adopted in the early empirical studies on the effect of inequality on growth. Most of these studies were carried out in the early 1990s. All of these found the effect to be *negative*. Higher inequality lowers the growth rate. A more recent cross-country analysis, Ostry et. al. (2014), using a new data set reaches the same conclusion.

Soon, however, it was realised that while inequality may have an effect on growth, it was unrealistic to think that growth depends *solely* on inequality. There obviously are a host of other factors that have a bearing on the growth rate of a country. In the simple cross-section framework with just the two variables (inequality and growth) in the picture, the effects of these other factors are not properly accounted for (or "controlled", to use a statistical term). Therefore, the estimate of the effect of inequality on growth that one gets under this approach may not be reliable. Moreover, we wish to have an idea about the signs of the effect in general rather than in a particular year.

For these reasons, starting from the late 1990s, researchers have hypothesised that the growth rate depends on a number of variables (including inequality) rather than on inequality alone and have sought to estimate the effects of all the different determinants of the growth rate by means of what is known as the *time series panel data technique*. This approach studies the behaviour of the variables *over time for a given sample of countries*, thus achieving some sort of an integration of the cross-section and the time series approaches. Progress in this direction has been aided by the recent advances (some of which we reviewed in Chapter 2) in constructing time series on inequality indices (such as the Gini coefficient) for a larger number of countries.

The overall findings of the studies that were carried out in the late 1990s and the 2000s on the basis of the panel data technique were in sharp contrast to those of the cross-section studies. The effect of inequality on economic growth was now found to be either negligible or *positive*. One important contribution to this line of research, Barro (2000), however, found that while this was true for the *full sample of countries*, that is, when *all* the countries in the sample are considered together. The picture changes if one distinguishes between low- and high-income countries. In low-income economies, inequality is, again, seen to have a *negative* effect on growth. It is, however, *positive* if the sample includes only the high-income countries. The dividing line between low- and high-income countries was put at a per capita GDP of $2070 (1985 US dollars). For a useful summary, displayed in a tabular form, of the findings of *all* the empirical studies dated up to the 2000s (including the earlier cross-section-based ones) regarding the sign of the effect of inequality on growth, see Cingano (2014, 37–39).

Research in this line, however, continues. It is now widely agreed that in less-developed economies, the effect of inequality on growth is negative. There is less agreement, however, over the sign of the effect in advanced economies. Cingano (2014) points out that most of the processes that make the sign of the effect of inequality on growth negative take time to work themselves out. Similar remarks apply to physical capital formation also if the investment projects have long gestation lags. Thus, it is the effect of inequality on *long-term* (rather than on short-term, for example, year-to-year) growth of the economy that should be expected to be negative. Cingano's own empirical study seems to conform this point. An analysis of the experience of the OECD countries showed that inequality (measured by the Gini) in a year had a *negative* impact on the average growth rate of the following five years. Since most of the OECD members are advanced economies, this implies that, contrary to the finding reported in Barro (2000), the effect of inequality has a negative sign even in the advanced world. Halter et. al. (2014) reach broadly similar conclusions. On the other hand, it is not surprising that Andrews et. al. (2011) who analysed annual data for 12 developed countries found a *positive* relation between the change in inequality and the change in the growth rate of the *immediately following year*. (These authors, however, measured inequality by top income shares rather than by the Gini coefficient.)

To summarise, in the empirical literature on the effect of inequality on growth there seems to be a broad agreement that in countries (such as India) with relatively low per capita incomes the effect has a negative sign. So far as the advanced economies are concerned, the sign seems to depend on whether one is talking about the effect on growth in the immediate future or about that in the longer run. In the former case, the sign may turn out to be positive or zero. In the latter case, however, it is, again, negative. Since the perspective of the Indian economy is of particular relevance in this book, it will henceforth be assumed that in a supply-constrained economy, inequality has an adverse impact on economic growth.

3.2.4 Effect of economic growth on inequality

3.2.4.1 The Kuznets curve: A digression

So far it is the effect of inequality on the rate of economic growth that has been at the centre of the discussion. It turns out, however, that there is also a causation in the reverse direction. The growth rate has an effect on the level of inequality in the distributions of income and wealth in the economy. It is now time to turn to this matter.

It should be mentioned at the outset of this discussion, however, that we are *not* talking here so much about the effect of the *level* of income (or output) on inequality. The effect of the per capita income level (i.e. the level of development of an economy) is a different issue and the subject of an old debate. The pioneering contribution in that line of research was that of Kuznets (1955) who analysed data relating to three advanced economies (USA, UK and Germany) and concluded that the pattern of the relation between inequality and income level has the shape of an "inverted U". As the income per capita increases, the level of inequality rises at first but starts falling after a certain level of income is reached. This is the famous "Kuznets curve". In more recent times, as data have been available for a much larger set of countries, however, the matter has been re-examined. The majority of researchers now seem to hold the opinion that there is no inverted U relation. Some hold the view that there is, in fact, a U-shaped relation, at least so far as the experience of the post-Second-World-War period is concerned, that is, in this period, as per capita income has increased, inequality has been seen to first fall and then rise. Some others deny the existence of any systematic relationship at all. On the other hand, Barro's (2000) time series panel data that has been referred to before seem to indicate that there is evidence for an inverted U curve even in the post-war period.

3.2.4.2 *Piketty's theory of inequality, the rate of return on capital and the growth rate*

Be that as it may, the main question here is whether the *rate of growth* of an economy exerts a systematic influence on the prevailing level of inequality of wealth and income and, if so, whether the effect is negative or positive in sign. The answers to these questions that will be given here are based on Piketty's (2014) well-known work. Piketty uses the terms *wealth* and *capital* interchangeably. Strictly speaking, there is a difference between the two. The wealth of a person (or an institution) is measured by net worth (i.e. the value of assets minus that of liabilities). The wealth of a country is simply the sum of the wealth of all persons and institutions (including the government) in the country. While in popular parlance, the wealth of a person is often called his or her capital, in economic theory capital is more often taken to be a factor of production which, together with land, labour and intermediate inputs, produces outputs. Piketty uses the word *capital* to mean *all* non-labour inputs in the production process. In this framework, capital and wealth are essentially the same notions. (There are still some subtle differences. For instance, an art treasure owned by a person is a part of the person's wealth but is not used in the production process. We shall, however, follow Piketty in assuming that these differences are quantitatively negligible and that wealth is essentially the same thing as capital.)

We shall also use the fact that the total income of an economy is the same thing as the total output. Start, now, by considering the question what would be the wealth–income (or, equivalently, the capital–output) ratio. Let K denote the capital stock and Y the level of output. By "equilibrium" (or "steady state") of an economy we shall mean the state of affairs in which all the important macroeconomic aggregates (such as K and Y) would change, if they change at all, *at the same rate* so that their ratios remain unchanged. Now, let g denote the proportional annual growth rate of total output Y (i.e. that of total income). Let s denote the average propensity to save, that is, the proportion of total income Y that is saved every year. Assume that whatever is saved is invested. Investment in a year is then sY. This, then, is the amount by which capital stock grows in a year. The proportional annual growth rate of capital stock, therefore, is sY/K. Now, if the capital–output ratio K/Y is to remain unchanged, this must also be the growth rate of the output. Hence, it is *necessary* that $g = s$Y/K, that is, K/Y $= s/g$. It is also easily seen that that this is a *sufficient* condition for steady state, that is, that if K/Y happens to be equal to s/g, then it will remain the same in the future and will be the steady state capital–output ratio.

In fact, something more is true. It can be shown, under some realistic assumptions, that the steady state capital–output ratio is *stable*, that is, that even if the economy starts from a situation where K/Y is *not* equal to s/g, it will converge to this value over time. The proof of this fact is a bit technical and we skip it here. (The interested reader may see the mathematical notes in Piketty (2014)).

The stability result implies that, if we observe an economy over a long period of time, the economy will be in the steady state most of the time. (As the famous economist Paul Samuelson was reported to be fond of saying, "How many times have you seen an egg stand on its head?"). Thus, in an empirical study of an economy over a long run, we can, for all practical purposes, proceed as though s/g is the *actual* capital–output ratio. The values of the parameters s and g, however, may change over time. If they do, so will the steady state capital–output ratio.

What is the relevance of all this for inequality of income distribution? First, consider the *functional* income distribution, that is, the distribution of total income between broad groups of people who perform different types of functions in the productive process. In particular, consider the division of total income between the owners of wealth (i.e. capital) whose function is to supply capital and the workers who supply the work effort and who own a negligible part of the capital stock. Let r denote the rate of return on capital. The wealth-owners' income is then rK so that their proportional share in total income is rK/Y. The percentage share is $(r$K/Y$) \times 100$.

Piketty and his collaborators undertook an ambitious research programme of estimating the functional distribution of income in the *global* economy as whole for a very long series of years spanning more than two centuries. By amassing and analysing a huge amount of data mostly for the advanced economies and supplementing these with as much information about other economies as was available, they calculated the capital–output ratio s/g for a long series of years. It was seen that this ratio was about 4.5 in 2010. It was apprehended, however, that it will rise to about 6.5 in the later decades of the twenty-first century (since g was expected to fall from its present level of more than 2 per cent to one of about 1.5 per cent while s was expected to remain more or less around its present value of about 10 per cent).

To get the wealth-owners' share in income, we have to multiply the capital–output ratio by r. Piketty's detailed empirical research found that historically r has mostly been around a central value of 4 to 6 per cent per year. There has been no pronounced trend either upward or downward. (In the very long-run spanning centuries, it may, however, have decreased slightly). Now, if we assume r to be 5 per cent, then, on the basis of the values of s/g mentioned above, it is seen that in the present times, the wealth-owners have a proportional share of about 22.5 per cent in total income and that the share may rise to 32.5 per cent in the later decades of the present century. Workers' share is about 77.5 per cent presently and may *fall* to 67.5 per cent. Even the present state of affairs, therefore, points towards a high degree of inequality in the functional income distribution since, as we have seen in Chapter 2, the major part of wealth is owned by a small proportion of the total population.

Moreover, income from wealth is more highly concentrated among the rich than income from labour. In other words, a person with high income usually gets the major part of his or her income from wealth rather than from labour. For this reason, the larger the share of wealth income in total income, the more unequal is the distribution of personal income in the economy.[7]

Consider now the question of our main concern viz. what happens to inequality when the growth rate changes. Since both r (which has always been in the vicinity of 5 per cent) and s (which is about 10 per cent and is expected to remain so in the future) may be treated as constants, a fall in g will imply a rise in $rs/g = r$K/Y which is the wealth share in total income. In view of the remarks in the previous paragraph, it immediately follows that inequality of income distribution in the economy will increase. Similarly, an increase in the growth rate will reduce income inequality. Thus, the effect of the growth rate on income inequality has a negative sign.

The same is also true of the effect of growth on *wealth inequality*. Piketty's research highlights the fact that r has always been greater than g. He emphasises that there is no logical reason why this needs to be the case. Rather, this is a historical fact. Piketty and Zucman (2015) proved that, under some assumptions, wealth inequality is governed by $r - g$. The fact that r exceeds g implies that $r - g$ is positive. Hence, there is always a positive degree of wealth inequality. Moreover, since r is nearly constant, a fall in g will increase $r - g$ and will, therefore, increase wealth inequality.[8]

3.2.5 A vicious circle

It is now clear that in a supply-constrained economy, the relation between high inequality and slow economic growth constitutes a vicious circle. While growth depends not only on the inequality of income and wealth in the economy but also on many other things, an increase in inequality, other things remaining the same, will reduce the growth rate. This is especially true if we focus attention on the rate of growth in the long run. The fall in the growth rate, in turn, will increase inequality even further. Thus, the increase in inequality will be a self-feeding process. For an economy (such as that of India) for which the need for economic growth cannot be overemphasised, breaking out of the vicious circle is an overriding necessity.

The silver lining is that the circularity operates in the reverse direction also. If inequality can be reduced, the vicious circle can be transformed into a virtuous one. The fall in inequality will raise the long-run growth rate which, in turn, will reduce inequality even further and so on.

3.3 Inequality and economic growth in a demand-constrained economy

3.3.1 Effect of inequality on growth

Turn now from the case of a supply-constrained economy to that of a demand-constrained one. The effect of inequality on economic growth in such an economy is, again, negative. The reasons for this are fairly obvious. Since demand deficiency, rather than lack of productive capacity, is now the constraint on the growth of output, it is obviously the effect of inequality on demand that is the essence of the matter. Now, aggregate demand in an economy consists of *four* parts. One part of demand comes from *consumption* by the people, sometimes called *private consumption*. A second part is *investment* which is the part of output that the producers use for the purpose of adding to their capital stock. A third part is *government expenditure* which measures the government's demand for goods and services (including the services of its employees) for the purpose of running the administration and for implementing various other programmes. The fourth part is demand from foreign sources measured by exports. However, since a country also *imports* goods and services from abroad and these are parts of the *supply* of the goods and services available in the economy rather than those of demand, it is *net exports* (i.e. exports minus imports) that is to be considered in this context.

In most countries, it is consumption that is the largest part of demand. (In India, it is presently (2022–23) close to 60 per cent of aggregate expenditure in the economy). Now, an increase in inequality reduces consumption (and, therefore, aggregate demand) in the economy. This is because the *propensity to consume* (i.e. the proportion of income that is spent on consumption) of a richer person is lower than that of a poorer one. Greater inequality implies a greater concentration of income in the hands of the relatively rich. A rise in inequality will, therefore, reduce *total demand* in the economy even at the same level of total income. If demand deficiency is what is restricting the growth of output, the problem obviously would get worse.

It is *investment*, however, that is the prime mover of growth. How inequality will affect investment is, therefore, the really important question here. The answer, however, emerges directly from the effect of inequality on demand. Investment adds to the productive capacity. Producers, therefore, are inclined to make investments only if they are confident that they would be able to sell the increased output made possible by the investment. The fall in total demand caused by the rise in inequality, therefore, will actually induce them to *reduce* the rate of investment. This will reduce the rate of economic growth. Similarly, a decrease in inequality will increase consumption demand (and, therefore, total demand) and will induce producers to increase investment. The growth rate will increase. Thus, in a demand-constrained economy, the effect of inequality on growth is negative.

Note also that, unlike in the case of supply-constrained economies, this will now be true of all economies, whether less developed or advanced, since, as noted above, consumption is the major part of total demand in about all the countries of the world. Moreover, the effect will make itself felt even in the short run, either instantaneously or with a short time gap of one year or less. (Needless to say, the effect will endure in the long run as well). This, too, is in contrast to the supply-constrained case where, as we have seen above, some of the important channels through which the negative effect of inequality on growth operates (for instance, the channel of human capital formation) take time to work.

3.3.2 The effect of growth on inequality

The effect of growth on inequality, however, is now a little more complex than in the case of the steady state analysis of supply-constrained economies discussed in Section 3.2.4. Note first, however, that it is still true that a fall in the growth rate will increase inequality. One of the main channels through which this effect operates is related to the *rate of unemployment*. It is obvious that if the unemployment rate (i.e. the proportion of the population with zero income) increases, then inequality *among* workers will increase because there will be greater concentration of the workers at zero income.[9] Now, since it is the workers that constitute the overwhelming majority of the population, empirically inequality *among workers* is seen to be responsible for the major part of the *overall* inequality of income in an economy. It is, therefore, reasonable to assert that the direction of change of overall inequality will be the same as that of inequality among workers.

Note that the rate of *employment* is L/P where L is the number of employed workers and P is population. Obviously, L/P will fall over time if the rate at which L increases (i.e. the rate of creation of new jobs) is less than the rate of population growth.

Now, a fall in the rate of economic growth (i.e. in the growth rate of total income in the economy) will induce the producers to *reduce* investment (possibly after a short time gap) since investment (which in addition to productive capacity) depends on the producers' expectations regarding the rate at which income (and, therefore, demand) is going to increase in future and since *expectations* about *future* growth rates are very frequently formed by looking at the *current* growth rates.

Since it is investment that creates new jobs, the fall in the growth rate will reduce the growth rate of L. Hence, even if we assume that initially L and P were growing at the same rate so that L/P was constant, it will now fall since the growth rate of population P is not affected. Thus, the rate of *unemployment* increases. Note also that if P was rising faster than L to start with so that the employment rate was already declining, the rising trend in the rate of unemployment will only be strengthened now. Inequality, therefore, will increase. We conclude that a fall in the growth rate of output or income is inequality-increasing.

Together with the fact (established in the previous subsection) that an increase in inequality reduces the growth rate, this implies that any increase in inequality will, again, set a vicious circle to work. An initial rise in inequality will reduce the growth rate which will increase inequality even further and so on.

There is, however, a subtle but important difference here from the case of a supply-constrained economy. While a *rise* in inequality will set off a *vicious* circle, there is now no certainty that a *fall* in inequality will set off a *virtuous* circle. While it *may* do so, there is no guarantee that it always will. To see why, one only has to look again at the behaviour of L/P over time. An initial fall in inequality will raise the growth rate in the short run which will increase investment and, therefore, the rate of new job creation. The growth rate of L will increase (possibly in the next period). But there will be no guarantee that the rate of employment L/P will be higher. It is possible that initially population P was rising faster than L and that even after the growth rate of L increases, the new (higher) growth rate of L is still lower than the growth rate of P. If that is the case, then L/P will continue to fall, that is, the rate of unemployment (and, therefore, inequality) will increase (in the next period). This *may* outweigh the *initial* decrease in inequality, preventing the process of falling inequality from being a self-propelling one.

One way of ensuring that a reduction in inequality would indeed be self-sustaining would be to bring down the rate of growth of population. For instance, it is obvious that if P is constant (as it nearly is in many of the advanced economies), then an initial reduction in inequality will, again, start a virtuous circle.

3.4 Conclusion

This chapter has shown that there are *economic* reasons why one should be interested in the issue of inequality. An increase in inequality has an adverse effect on the rate of economic growth. This is true irrespective of whether the economy is supply or demand constrained. Moreover, there is a vicious circle here in the sense that a rising trend in inequality and a falling trend in the growth rate would reinforce each other. In a supply-constrained economy, there is also a virtuous circle in the sense that a *fall* in inequality and *rising* growth rate would reinforce each other, at least in the long run. In a demand-constrained economy, there is, again, a vicious circle of the type stated above. While the virtuous circle of falling inequality and rising growth rate cannot now be proved in the general case, a decrease in inequality would, again, unambiguously increase the short-run growth rate. Moreover, if the rate of population growth is low enough, then the virtuous circle, too, would be operative again. Overall, since the importance of growth for an economy such as that of India hardly needs any elaboration, we have a case for believing that a reduction in inequality would be desired not only on the moral ground but also on the economic one.

Notes

1 The output of an *individual* producer, of course, would also involve the use of *intermediate inputs* purchased from *other* producers. We are, however, talking here about the *aggregate* output of an economy.
2 One empirical study of an Indian village in 1990 reported an average rate of interest of 78.5 per cent per annum in the informal credit market. See World Bank (2006, 90). At the time, the lending rate of banks was about 18 per cent per annum on average.
3 An earlier contribution, Althaus (1980), had also discussed the relation between fertility differentials and economic growth. However, in that contribution, the argument was not extended to the relation between inequality and economic growth. Moreover, fertility differentials were considered to be exogenously given rather than determined by income differences. The crucial role of human capital formation and its relation with fertility differences were also not brought into the picture.
4 If the number of persons, n, is even, an income distribution may have more than one median. One way of breaking the tie would be to consider the arithmetic average of the different median incomes to be *the* median.
5 In fact, for this reason, the excess of the mean income over the median income, expressed as the proportion of the mean income, is sometimes taken as an index of inequality of an income distribution. In the example used in the text, the value of this index is $(15 - 12)/15 = 0.20$.
6 What has been stated in the text is a simplified version of the median voter theorem. In its general form, the theorem does not assume that the choice is limited to just two alternatives. It does, however, make a number of other assumptions including the ones that for each voter there is a particular alternative that is the most preferred among all the alternatives and that all voters participate in the voting process (i.e. that there are no abstentions). The interested reader may see Meltzer and Richard (1981) and the references cited there.
7 The summary of Piketty's arguments provided here owes much to Robert Solow's review of Piketty's (2014) book. See Solow (2014).

8 Hiraguchi (2019) shows that Piketty and Zucman's conclusions in this regard are robust. They survive even if some of the assumptions are relaxed.
9 In practice, workers who do not find formal jobs seek employment in what is called the *informal sector*. This, however, does not alter the argument in the text substantially as long as a worker's income from the informal sector is less than the wage rate in the formal sector.

References

Aisen, A. and Veiga, F.J. (2013): "How does political instability affect economic growth?", *European Journal of Political Economy*, Vol. 29, 151–167.

Alesina, A. and Perotti, R. (1996): "Income distribution, political instability and investment", *European Economic Review*, Vol. 81, 1170–1189.

Alesina, A. and Rodrik, D. (1994): "Distribution politics and economic growth", *Quarterly Journal of Economics*, Vol. 109, 465–490.

Althaus, P.G. (1980): "Differential fertility and economic growth", *Zeitschrift fur die gesamte Staatwissenschaft*, Vol. 136, 309–326.

Andrews, D., Jencks, C. and Leigh, A. (2011): "Do rising top incomes lift all boats?", *The B.E. Journal of Economic Analysis & Policy*, Vol. 11, 1–45.

Banerjee, A.V. and Newman, A.F. (1993): "Occupational choice and the process of development", *Journal of Political Economy*, Vol. 101, 274–298.

Barro, R.J. (2000): "Inequality and growth in a panel of countries", *Journal of Economic Growth*, Vol. 5, 5–32.

Benhabib, J. and Rustichini, A. (1996): "Social conflict and growth", *Journal of Economic Growth*, Vol. 1, 129–146.

Bertola, G. (1993): "Factor shares and savings in endogenous growth", *American Economic Review*, Vol. 83, 1184–1198.

Bourguignon, F. (1981): "Pareto superiority of unegalitarian equilibria in Stiglitz' model of wealth distribution with convex saving function", *Econometrica*, Vol. 49, 1469–1475.

Cingano, F. (2014): "Trends in income inequality and its effect on economic growth", OECD Social. Employment and Migration Working Papers, No. 163, Organization for Economic Cooperation and Development, Paris.

De la Croix, D. and Doepke, M. (2003): "Inequality and growth: why differential fertility matters", *American Economic Review*, Vol. 93, 1091–1113.

Galor, O. and Zeira, J. (1993): "Income distribution and macroeconomics", *Review of Economic Studies*, Vol. 60, 35–52.

Hadzi-Vascov, M., Pienknagura, S. and Ricci, L.A. (2021): "The Macroeconomic Impact of Social Unrest", IMF Working Paper No. WP/21/135, International Monetary Fund, Washington DC.

Halter, D., Oechslin, M. and Zweimuller, J. (2014): "Inequality and growth: The neglected time dimension", *Journal of Economic Growth*, Vol. 19, 81–104.

Hiraguchi, R. (2019): "Wealth inequality, or $r - g$, in the economic growth model", *Macroeconomic Dynamics*, Vol. 23, 479–488.

Kaldor, N. (1955): "Alternative theories of distribution", *Review of Economic Studies*, Vol. 23, 83–100.

Keynes, J.M. (1920): *The Economic Consequences of the Peace*, Harcourt, Brace and Howe, New York.

Kremer, M. and Chen, D. (2002): "Income distribution dynamics and endogenous fertility", *Journal of Economic Growth*, Vol. 7, 227–258.

Kuznets, S. (1955): "Economic growth and income inequality", *American Economic Review*, Vol. 45, 1–28.

Lewis, W.A. (1954): "Economic development with unlimited supply of labour", *The Manchester School*, Vol. 22, 139–191.

Loury, G., (1981): "Intergenerational transfers and the distribution of earnings", *Econometrica*, Vol. 49, 843–867.

Meltzer, A.H. and Richard, S.F. (1981): "A rational theory of the size of government", *Journal of Political Economy*, Vol. 89, 914–927.

Milanovic, B. (2000): "The median voter hypothesis, income inequality and income redistribution: An empirical test with the required data", *European Journal of Political Economy*, Vol. 16. 367–410.

Ostry, J.D., Berg, A. and Tsangarides, C.G. (2014): *Redistribution, Inequality* and *Growth, IMF Staff Discussion Note*, International Monetary Fund, Washington DC.

Perotti, R. (1993): "Political equilibrium, income distribution and growth", *Review of Economic Studies*, Vol. 60, 755–776.

Persson, T. and Tabellini, G. (1994): "Is inequality harmful for growth? Theory and evidence", *American Economic Review*, Vol. 84, 600–621.

Piketty, T. (2014): *Capital in the Twenty-First Century*, Harvard University Press, Cambridge, MA.

Piketty, T. and Zucman, G. (2015): "Wealth and inheritance in the long run", in Atkinson, A.B. and Bourguignon, F. (eds.): *Handbook of Income Distribution*, Vol. II, Norh-Holland, Amsterdam, 1303–1368.

Solow, R.M. (2014): "Thomas Piketty is right", *The New Republic*, April 23, 2014, www.newrepublic.com last accessed on October 2, 2023.

United Nations. (2022): *World Population Prospects 2022: Release Note*, United Nations, Department of Economic and Social Affairs, Population Division, United Nations, New York.

World Bank. (2006): *World Development Report 2006*, World Bank. Washington DC.

4 The long-run sustainability of profits

4.1 Introduction

The previous chapters discussed in detail the rising trend of inequality and the reasons why inequality has an adverse effect on economic growth. It is now time to ask what, if anything, can be done to arrest the rising trend. One enters the realm of *policy*. In economic parlance, economic policy usually refers to actions that the *government* (or some other appropriate authority such as the central bank) can possibly take to fix an economic problem. This is certainly a very important topic of discussion. Much, however, has been written on the matter both in general terms and with particular reference to economic inequality in the Indian context. There is no dearth of books on these issues. (See, for instance, Banerjee (2023), Goyal (2019) and Kapila (2020)).

As was emphasised in Chapter 1, however, the focus of this book is not on the role of the government but on the role that decision-makers in the private business sector can play in this connection. As was noted there, this may sound a bit puzzling at first. In popular discourses, the blame for the inequality of income and wealth distributions is usually laid at the doors of private business. The unscrupulous pursuit of profit by private producers is often considered to be the main cause of the problem of inequality. This popular view is not entirely baseless either. In this book, however, we argue that business managers can play an important role in this context. They can serve their own interests *and* the broader economic interests of the country as a whole at the same time if they keep in mind two crucial aspects of the matter. One of these relates to the distinction between short- and long-run profit maximisation and the other to one between individual rationality and social rationality. This chapter discusses the first of these two issues. The second one will be taken up in Chapter 5.

Needless to say, it is a profit-making firm that can contribute to the economic growth of the country by using its profits for the purpose of investment. Fast economic growth leads to lower incidence of poverty and inequality. Clearly, therefore, profit-making firms can make significant

DOI: 10.4324/9781032707082-4

contributions to the twin problems of high economic inequality and slow economic growth that are the main concerns of this book. What, then, is the reason behind the view that it is "profit-mongering" on the part of private sector producers that is the common cause of both of these problems? In this chapter, it is argued that one resolution of this apparent paradox lies in recognising the crucial importance of the time horizon over which the profits of a firm are to be calculated. What is optimal for the maximisation of instantaneous profits is frequently seen to be non-optimal if it is profits over a longer run of time that is of concern. The basic message of this chapter is that it is in the best interests of both the economy of the country as a whole and a particular business firm that the firm adopts policies that are consistent with the objective of the maximisation of its long-run profits.

Section 4.2 starts with the universally accepted proposition that the objective of a business firm is (and should be) to maximise profit. It discusses a basic result of economic theory that states that, under some assumptions, the pursuit of self-interest on the part of every economic unit (such as a producer or a consumer) actually promotes *social* well-being. It is to be noted, however, that this is true only if it is assumed, *inter alia*, that it is the long-term interests of the economic units that we are talking about. We shall explain why this point is of particular relevance in a supply-constrained economy where the major limitation on the expansion of output comes from constraints on the available amounts and the productivities of the factors of production. We shall briefly discuss some cases in which the productivity of some non-human inputs (such as land and machinery) can suffer in the long run if firm managers take myopic decisions. The case of productivity of labour is taken up separately and in a little greater detail in Section 4.3 in view of its importance in the present context. Section 4.4 concludes the chapter.

4.2 Profit maximisation: The long run versus the short

4.2.1 Self-interest and the interests of the society: The First Theorem of Welfare Economics

It goes without saying that business managers would seek to maximise the profits of the firm that they manage. In fact, the economic philosophy of capitalism would claim that by doing so, the managers would be promoting the interests of not only the firm but also the larger interests of the economy and the society. The idea basically is that the aggregate well-being of an economy is maximised if and only if each economic decision-making unit, be it a producer or a consumer, seeks to promote his or her own interest. In particular, each consumer should maximise his or her own utility and each producer should maximise profit. Adam Smith is widely believed to be the first proponent of this notion. His book *An Inquiry into the Nature and Causes of the Wealth of Nations*, published originally in two volumes in 1776 and 1778, contained the first clear statement of the idea which is now considered to be a classic result and, indeed, the intellectual foundation of capitalism. (See Smith (1776, 1778)). It was much later, in the 1950s and 1960s, that it was mathematically proved that, contrary to what may seem to be the case, if everybody pursues his or her self-interest, the overall result is *not* total confusion. On the contrary, there will be harmony in the sense that there is a *general equilibrium* where demand and supply for every produced good as well as for every factor of production (including labour) would be equal. Moreover, it was proved that in a general equilibrium, the overall welfare of the society is maximised. This last proposition is known as the *First Theorem of Welfare Economics*.

Two things, however, need to be noted about this theorem. *First*, it is based on a large number of *assumptions*. In particular, the market for *every* commodity must be *perfectly competitive*. This is a rather demanding assumption and includes, in turn, a whole gamut of requirements. For instance, in each market there should be a *large number of producers as well as a large number of consumers*, there should be *free entry and exit* in each market (i.e. anybody who wants to produce any particular commodity is able to do so and any existing producer who wants to stop production is also able to do so), there should be *no asymmetry of information* between the economic units (i.e. nobody should have information that is not shared by everybody else), there should be *no uncertainty* and so on.[1]

Second, when it is claimed that the overall welfare of the society is maximised, there arises the question how overall welfare is to be calculated. One person's welfare may be taken to be the utility that the person derives from the goods and services that the person gets to consume. But how is the *aggregate* welfare of the society to be defined? The "sum of individual utilities" would not make sense not only because one person's utility is not comparable to another's (since, for instance, one person may be very fastidious and not easily satisfied while another may be easily pleased) but also because even one person's utility is not measurable by a cardinal number. I can only say, for instance, that my utility from one bundle of goods and services is, say, higher than my utility from another. It is difficult to describe by a number exactly how much satisfaction I get from a specific bundle. In other words, I can only *rank* different bundles in terms of my utility or preference. Since a person's utility is not a cardinal number, the "sum" of different persons' utilities would not be a meaningful concept even if utility *was* interpersonally comparable.

Because of the difficulties of measuring utility or welfare, the First Theorem of Welfare Economics uses the phrase "maximum overall welfare" in a specific sense based on the *ranking* property of individual utilities. What is claimed is that a general equilibrium is "Pareto optimal". To see what this means, consider two different specifications (denoted by A and B) of the utilities of the different persons. Now, situation A is said to be "Pareto-superior" to situation B if, in A, nobody's utility is less than what is in B and there is at least one individual whose utility is greater in A than in B. Note that we are not comparing anybody's utility with that of anybody else. Each person's utility in situation A is being compared only with his or her own utility in situation B. Thus, there is no interpersonal comparison of utility. Moreover, even for a given individual, we only need to know whether his or her utility in situation A is higher than (or lower than or the same as) what it is in situation B. We are only using the *ranking* of a person's utilities in different situations. Now, a given distribution of utilities in the society is called Pareto optimal if no other conceivable distribution is Pareto-superior. In other words, a given distribution of utilities is Pareto optimal if and only if it is the case that, starting from this situation, if we wish to *increase* the utility of any one individual, at least one other individual's utility must be *decreased*. (Otherwise, the other situation would be Pareto-superior so that the initial situation is not Pareto optimal). It is in this sense that if all the assumptions of the theory that we have referred to above are satisfied, then a general equilibrium of an economy is welfare-maximising.[2]

4.2.2 Short- and long-run profits

Adam Smith's original insight, together with its more modern statement in the form of the First Theorem of Welfare Economics, forms the basis of the notion that profit-seeking by private producers is actually conducive to the social good. Milton Friedman's famous statement that the *social* role of a firm is to earn profit summarises this view. There have been criticisms of this position. The usual source of these critiques is the long list of assumptions on which this view is based. For instance, if there is imperfect competition on the production side of a market (say, an oligopoly which is a situation where there are only a few producers of a commodity but a large number of consumers), then the producers will wield market power and use it to charge prices that will be higher than the price under perfect competition. While competitive price includes a normal rate of profit, oligopolistic prices would bring supernormal profits. The higher profits, however, do not signify a higher level of social welfare. The First Theorem of Welfare Economics no longer applies since one of its basic assumptions (viz. perfect competition) is violated.

We shall, however, focus here on a different issue in this connection. We argue that the amount of profit often depends on the time period over which profit is calculated. A business decision that is optimal for a firm from the point of view of maximisation of *short-run* profits is not necessarily optimal from a *long-run* viewpoint. Informally, the basic point here is that it is always enticing to make a "quick buck", but this often involves some hidden costs that make their presence felt only after a gap of time rather than immediately. Failure to take note of these costs while calculating profits would jeopardise the long-run interests of the firm itself. Needless to say, this will not lead to a social optimum either even if all the assumptions of the First Theorem of Welfare Economics are satisfied.

Before considering specific instances of this phenomenon, it is important to note that we are talking here about how the profit of a business firm is to be *calculated*. The difference between "properly" and "improperly" calculated profits is related to but not the same as the distinction between the short- and the long-run profits in the theory of price determination under perfect competition as it is usually presented in the textbooks of economics. In that theory, the number of firms in the market for a product is fixed in the short run. In the long run, however, it is variable since there is free entry and exit in the market. Now, if the market for a product is perfectly competitive, each producer will produce the commodity in such an amount as to equate price to the marginal cost (MC) of production which is the change in the cost of production when output changes (i.e. either increases or decreases) by one unit.[3] Moreover, *in the long run*, the price of the product would also have to be equal to the average cost (AC) of production which is simply the total cost of production divided by the output level. "Normal" profit is assumed to be included in the cost of production. This means that there would be no supernormal profits in the long run. This is because if any firm makes supernormal profits, this will attract new producers to enter the field. The forces of competition will push up input prices (so that AC rises) and push down the price at which the product can be sold in the market. Supernormal profits will decrease. They will continue to do so until the price equals AC.

What we are concerned with in the present context, however, is not so much the fact that some profits are supernormal and would be reduced to zero in the long run by the entry of new firms. Rather, it is that very often some business decisions seem to be profitable because profits are calculated by ignoring some costs that come to be noticed only in the long run. Thus, in the long run, the firm's profitability would be in jeopardy even if new firms do not enter the picture, that is, even if the market is not competitive.

4.2.3 Factor productivity and the supply-constrained economy: The non-labour factors

The type of problem that we are concerned with in this context is best illustrated by considering an economy that is *supply-constrained*. It is in such economies that the need to focus on long-term profits is particularly relevant. Growth in such economies obviously depends upon creating additional *capacity* to produce goods and services. The factors of production, therefore, are of crucial importance. Capital and labour are traditionally considered to be the two most important factors of production. For a country such as India where agriculture is an important part of the economy, land is also an important productive factor.[4] Now, the capacity to produce can be increased in two ways: increasing the quantities of the factors of production and by increasing their productivities (i.e. making each unit of the factors more efficient). In a supply-constrained economy, however, it is, by definition, the case that it is difficult to increase the supplies of the factors. It is the constraints on the factor supplies that make an economy supply-constrained. Moreover, apart from the distinction between supply- and demand-constrained economies, it is a matter of historical fact that in most countries economic growth has largely been due more to technological progress and the resultant increase in factor productivities than to increases in the available quantities of the factors. Robert Solow's classic paper (Solow (1957)) showed this for the economy of the USA.

In the discussion below, therefore, we concentrate on the issue of productivity. First, a word about the notion of productivity. While, conceptually, the productivity of a factor is the factor's own contribution towards output, in practice we define it simply as output divided by the amount of the factor and call this ratio the *average* productivity of the factor. From a theoretical viewpoint, the limitation of the definition should be obvious. Output is produced by the combination of all the factors of production. It is not the contribution of this factor alone in abstraction from that of the others. However, we shall follow the usual practice of working with this definition.[5] Thus, by labour productivity, for instance, we shall mean average productivity of labour, that is, output divided by the amount of labour employed where output is measured by real GDP (i.e. GDP at current prices deflated at an appropriate rate in order to take care of inflation).

How to *maintain* and, if possible, *increase* factor productivity are vital questions from the viewpoint of economic growth. Consider maintenance and consider first the case of non-human factors such as land and machinery. The factors depreciate through the normal process of wear and tear. This is most obvious in agricultural production where the productivity of land is a crucial matter. The nutrients of the soil are depleted by the very process of cultivation. That is why in old-fashioned agriculture it was standard practice for a farmer to keep the plot of land (or a part of it) fallow for a year after it had been used constantly for a number of years. This would restore the fertility of the land in a natural way. In modern agriculture, however, the need for this practice is often disregarded. As a result, productivity per hectare of land is often seen to be decreasing over time. This has obvious repercussions on profit. If the concern is exclusively with this year's profit, it is possible that at the prices that are expected to prevail in the market for the produce (or at the prices offered by government procurement programmes), a particular production plan would be profitable. From the point of view of a longer-time horizon (of, say, five or ten years), however, the profit calculations must take cognisance of the decline in the productivity of land over time caused by constant use. Nowadays, one hardly sees the practice of giving periodic rest to the plots under cultivation. Therefore, there arises the need for increasingly heavier doses of investment in terms of fertilisers, irrigation and other inputs in order to compensate for the decline in the fertility of land. Even if it is assumed that it is possible to maintain profits in this way, there would be the need to redo the profit calculations. Clearly, there is a disjunction between short- and long-run profits. Moreover, there is a limit on how long the long-term fall in profitability can be delayed in this fashion. In particular, if irrigation is based on groundwater, increasingly intensive use of groundwater resources would, in course of time, severely erode the reserves of such water. This, in fact, has happened in Indian agriculture. In the 1970s, the Green Revolution led to a spurt in the growth rates of wheat and other cereals. Over the decades, however, there has been a gradual deceleration of the agricultural growth rate. In some areas in the northern and the north-western states where the Green Revolution was initially extremely successful in expanding output, the output per hectare of land has dwindled in recent decades. (See, for instance, the discussion in Sasmal (2016, Chapter 4)).

While land productivity may be a relatively unimportant issue in sectors other than agriculture, the general distinction between short- and long-run profit maximisation has economy-wide significance. There are costs that would need to be borne at a future point of time. If a firm is concerned only with its profits in the immediate future, it would tend to ignore such costs. One specific instance that bears similarity to the decline in the fertility of land over time relates to the physical wear and tear of fixed capital. Buildings and machinery depreciate over time. It is true that, unlike in the case of agricultural land, this decline in the productive potential of the inputs over time is supposed to be taken into consideration when profit is calculated for official records. Depreciation is treated as a cost item (as it should be) while arriving at the profit figure for the purpose of accounting and for filing income tax returns. It is, however, seldom the case in practice that the firm actually maintains a separate depreciation fund where each year's depreciation is deposited and refrains from using this fund for any purpose other than replacing a fixed capital equipment at the end of its working life. More often, the end of the working life of an equipment is considered to be an event that is too remote to be bothered about at the present moment. The firm often behaves as if the *gross profit* (i.e. profit before taking account of depreciation cost) was the true profit. This, in turn, leads to wrong business decisions and would reduce even gross profits in the long run when the working life of the equipment comes to an end.

So far we have only talked about *maintaining* the productivity of land and machines. Needless to say, if the economy is to grow over time, it is also necessary to *increase* their productivity. It is easy to see that to make a factor more productive (i.e. to make it more efficient by enabling one unit of the factor to produce a greater amount of output) what is needed is investment. The investment will often take the form of employing greater amounts of *other* inputs. What needs to be remembered, however, is that the investment needs to be of the appropriate *type*. For instance, consider, again, the case of land in agriculture. We have noted before that to *maintain* its fertility a plot of land has to be periodically kept fallow. To *increase* its productivity, however, we need to invest in land. What can "investment in land" mean? One possibility for an *individual* farmer is to purchase (or rent) more land. Recall again, however, that we are talking about a supply-constrained economy so that it is not possible for all farmers to increase the quantity of land used. In fact, a special feature of land as a factor of production is that its total supply in an economy is fixed.[6] One feasible alternative is to increase fertility by heavier doses of fertilisers. The choice of appropriate types of investment becomes relevant here. It is now well-documented that heavier doses of chemical fertilisers do not necessarily lead to sustainable increase in fertility in the long run. What is needed is an optimal combination of chemical and biological fertilisers. Note that the opposition between the short- and the long-run perspectives makes its appearance again. It is possible to achieve a dramatic increase in output per hectare of land in the immediate future by investing heavily in chemical fertilisers. It is in the longer run that the deleterious effect on fertility would make itself felt.

In this respect, the case of machinery and equipment is a little different. Once a machine is installed, its productive capacity is fixed. Therefore, if it is used at full capacity, it is not possible to increase its productivity in the usual sense of the term even if greater amounts of other inputs (such as labour and raw materials) are harnessed to work with the machine. In practice, however, there is scope for increasing long-term (as opposed to short term) profits of the firm by paying greater attention to proper *usage* of the machine. There is always a maximum workload that a machine can take. This load is maximal in the sense that if this limit is exceeded, the machine would break down physically and putting it back to work would involve heavy expenses. Frequently, in that case, it would need to be replaced by a new machine altogether. However, apart from the *physical* maximum capacity, in practice, there is often a recommended *operational* maximum which is usually less than the physical maximum. The difference between the two is that while it is desirable to keep the workload within the bounds of the operational maximum, it is not the case that it cannot be exceeded for short periods of time. If it is exceeded for *prolonged* periods, however, there would be risk of a break down. The physical maximum, on the other hand, cannot be exceeded even for a short duration of time without causing a breakdown. The relevance of this distinction in our present context is that since the operational maximum can be exceeded for some time without precipitating an immediate breakdown, for a firm that is concerned only with its immediate profits, it would be tempting to increase production by exceeding the operational limit. (Recall again that in this chapter we are assuming that there is no demand problem i.e. that the increased output can always be sold). The problem is that since this is true at every point of time, there is a strong possibility that violation of the operational limit would go on indefinitely, eventually causing a total breakdown of the machine and endangering the long-term profits of the firm.

4.3 Labour productivity, wages and inequality

4.3.1 Effect of the wage rate on labour productivity: Brassey's Law

The case of labour productivity merits a separate discussion. The first thing to be noted in this connection is that there is a relation between labour productivity and the wage rate in a firm. This is the subject of this subsection.

Start by noting that the output of a firm is measured by its *value added* (i.e. the market value of the produced goods and services minus the value of intermediate inputs). After the products are sold in the market, the value added is used to pay wages to workers. The rest is profit. Thus, value added is essentially wages plus profit. Assume for simplicity that profits are used by the firms for the purpose of adding to the firm's capital, that is, for making the firm *grow*.

It is obvious that at any given point of time, there would be a negative relationship between total wages (i.e. the wage bill) paid by a firm and its profits. The higher is the wage bill, the lower are profits and vice versa. In fact, this is also usually true of the wage *rate* (i.e. the wage paid to each worker) and the *rate* of profit (i.e. the amount of profit divided by the value of capital invested). Capital is invested at the beginning of the production process. This is true of both *fixed capital* such as machinery and equipment and *circulating* (or *working*) *capital* such as expenditure on raw materials and other intermediate inputs. Profit, however, is calculated *after* the output has been produced and sold. Labour is also paid *post factum* (i.e. at the end of the process) although the wage rate is negotiated at the beginning, right after the firm has formulated its production plan and decided on the amount of labour to be employed. Thus, when profits are calculated, both the amount of capital invested and the quantity of labour employed are given. The wage rate (that was decided at the beginning of the production process) will, thus, be inversely related to the rate of profit that would be known only after the end of the process.

A business decision-maker seeking to maximise profits would seek to minimise wages. While there is nothing wrong with this from the viewpoint of the objective of the firm, the problem, again, comes from the tension between short- and long-run profits.

The point needs some elaboration. The low average productivity of the workers is frequently caused by low levels of investment in human capital. In many of the less-developed countries, it is not only the education and training of the children but also their nutritional requirements that are neglected. On the other hand, the beneficial effect of higher wages on labour efficiency was noted way back in the second half of the nineteenth century in the-then fast-industrialising Britain. Practical businessmen such as Thomas Brassey noticed what was then considered an "unusual" phenomenon. As they paid their workers higher wages, a *more than proportionate* increase in output per worker seemed to be elicited. Later, this came to be known as Brassey's Law in Britain and as the theory of the "economy of high wages" in the USA. Since then both economists and experienced businessmen have repeatedly referred to the phenomenon. Adam Smith's *Wealth of Nations* contained the sentence, "When wages are high, accordingly we shall always find the workmen more active, diligent and expeditious than where they are low". (See Smith (1776, 86)). Henry Ford followed a very liberal wage policy in his Ford Motor Company and used to emphasise that he was doing so in the long-run interest of the company itself and not just as an act of philanthropy. The idea is closely related to what has been called the "nutrition model" in the more recent academic literature on the theory of economic development. See, for instance, Bliss and Stern (1978) and Dasgupta and Roy (1986, 1987). On Brassey's Law, see Petridis (1996).

All this has a direct relationship with the wage policies followed by the firms. Minimising wages may increase the firms' short-run profits. In the *long run*, however, the resulting ill health and lack of basic education causes low levels of labour efficiency and constrains the profit and growth possibilities of the firms and, therefore, also the growth possibilities of the economy as a whole.

4.3.2 Weak effect of labour productivity on wage: The Indian case

While rising wages are frequently seen to increase labour productivity, it is by no means the case that a rising trend in labour productivity always induces a rising trend in real wages. India is a case in point. In recent decades, average labour productivity in India has, indeed, increased at a reasonably high rate, at least in comparison to that in many other economies. However, the rate of growth of real wages has failed to keep pace with labour productivity. This has tended to increase inequality and threatens to constrain the long-run growth possibilities of the country.

In this context, we look at the observed time patterns of growth of (average) labour productivity and the growth of wages in India. Needless to say, it is real wages (i.e. money wages divided by the price level) that is important here because it is the real purchasing power of the workers that matters.[7] If the rate of inflation exceeds the rate of growth of money wages, there will be a fall in the real standard of living of the workers in spite of the increase in money wages.

Even in the year 2020, when COVID-19 was raging in full fury in the country, labour productivity in India grew at a rate of more than 2 per cent over the preceding year. In the following year, it grew at the rate of more than 3.5 per cent. The record looks even better if we consider the past three decades. Over the period from 1992 to 2021, labour productivity in India grew at an average annual rate of about 4.4 per cent. (www.ceicdata.com/en/indicator/india/labour-productivity-growth last accessed on July 3, 2023). These growth figures stand out to be quite impressive if we compare them not only with the corresponding figures for most other South Asian economies but also with those for advanced economies such as the USA. Average labour productivity in the USA grew at an average rate of 3.2 per cent between 1950 and 1970. In the period from 1970 and 1990, this average rate fell to 1.9 per cent. Subsequently, however, it has improved. The average rate of annual increase over the period from 1991 to the present is 2.3 per cent.

Compared to the labour productivity growth rate, however, the rate of growth of real wages in India is quite low. Over the period from 2014–15 to 2021–22, the average annual growth rate of real wages in India was less than 1 per cent. These are overall estimates considering all the sectors of the economy. In many important sectors, the figures were lower than even this low average rate. For instance, in manufacturing and construction, the average annual growth rates were just 0.3 per cent and 0.2 per cent respectively. In agriculture, it was 0.9 per cent. It has been rightly remarked by Dreze (2023) that "there has been no significant growth of real wages at the all-India level in the last eight years". It is little consolation that the situation in other countries is not much different. (See, for instance, van Briesbroeck (2015)).

At this point, one may ask how it is at all possible that real wage differs from labour productivity if firms are profit maximisers. To maximise profit, a firm must employ labour in an amount such that real wage *equals* marginal productivity of labour. Marginal productivity, in turn, would equal average productivity in the long run under perfect competition. Hence, average labour productivity must be the same as the real wage rate, at least in the long run.[8]

This argument, however, is valid only under the assumption that the market is perfectly competitive. Recall our discussion of the First Theorem of Welfare Economics where we saw how stringent these assumptions are. There are, therefore, many reasons why in reality the real wage rate is frequently less than labour productivity. In any industry, the large firms wield considerable market power. They do not play a perfectly competitive game. In particular, they do not take the output price and the prices of the factors of production (including the wage rate) as given. Unlike in the model of perfect competition where each firm is too small a part of the market to influence the output and input prices by its unilateral action, a large firm can influence these prices by changing its output and its employment of the factors of production. This is most obvious in the case where the firm in question is a monopoly. The same is, however, also true in the more usual case of oligopoly where there are only a handful of large firms in an industry. In such markets, the output and input prices are not given data so far as the firms are concerned. The firms set all of these prices themselves so as to maximise profits. In such markets, the output prices are higher and input prices are lower than what these would be in a perfectly competitive market. The wage rate would be typically less than the *marginal* productivity of labour. Moreover, it is possible for such firms to use their market power to reduce the wage rate to a level below the *average* productivity of labour so that the firm earns supernormal profits. They would do so even in the long run since the forces of perfect competition would not be there to ensure that new firms would enter the market and eventually all supernormal profits would be competed away.

How significant is the degree of market imperfection in the Indian economy? Various measures of such imperfection are available. As we have seen before, under perfect competition a firm decides to produce that level of output at which price of the output equals the MC of production (i.e. the increase in the cost of production when output changes by a small amount). In imperfect competition, however, the output price charged by the firm exceeds MC. Therefore, one suggested measure of the degree of imperfection is the proportion (or percentage) by which the price exceeds the MC. There are also other measures that are obtained from the statistical size distributions of firms. Just as the Gini index mentioned in Chapter 2 measures the inequality of the distribution of personal (or household) incomes in an economy, there is the so-called Herfindahl–Hirschman index of concentration, based on a formula that essentially measures the inequality of the distribution firm sizes. If there are only a few large firms accounting for the lion's share of the total output, the index will have a high value.

It will have a low value if there are a large number of firms each of which contributes a negligible percentage of the total output. This is related to yet another approach based on the size distributions of firms. Here, the idea is to measure the degree of *positive skewness* of the distribution. Intuitively, a firm size distribution is called positively skewed if there is a preponderance of small-sized firms while there are only a few firms of large size.

All of these indices can be applied at various levels of aggregation. One can talk about the concentration of market power in a specific industry or in a specific sector of the economy or in the economy as a whole.

While estimates of the concentration of market power in the Indian economy as a whole are hard to come by, there are some estimates of *industrial* concentration. Sedai (2016) reports that the size distribution of firms in the *manufacturing* sector of the Indian economy became more positively skewed over the period from 1999 to 2013. Saraswati (2019) found that in a number of subsectors of the manufacturing sector, both the Herfindahl–Hirschman index of concentration and the degree of market imperfection measured by the excess of price over MC were *significantly higher* in the period 2014–17 than during 2009–14. It was, however, also true that in some other subsectors there was a *slight fall* in these measures of concentration. It was also noted that by conventional standards, the absolute value of the overall degree of market imperfection in the *industrial sector* as a whole (which includes manufacturing) has remained high in India over several decades.

It is not surprising that in such a scenario, business decision-makers would be tempted to use their market power to hold the growth rate of real wages below the rate of growth of labour productivity. It is easy to see, however, that it is only in the short run that this would serve their interests. Since GDP can be written as the value of total output in the economy, PY, where P and Y are, respectively, measures of the general price level and output in the economy as a whole, the share of labour in GDP is WL/PY, where W is the money wage rate and L is employment. It is easily seen that WL/PY = (W/P)/(Y/L) = (the real wage rate)/(average labour productivity). Hence, if the growth rate of the real wage rate over time is less than that of labour productivity, then labour's share in GDP would decline. This is precisely what has been happening in the Indian economy over the last few decades. Since labourers (as opposed to the owners of capital) constitute the majority of the population, it is no wonder that inequality in the distribution of income in the economy as a whole has increased as was seen in Chapter 2. Recall that in a supply-constrained economy (which is the case under consideration in the present chapter), inequality of income distribution would constrain the rate of growth in the economy at least in the long run as was seen in Chapter 3.

4.3.3 The positive effect of economic growth on firm performance

Now comes the last link in the chain of arguments. It consists of the following fact. *Business firms thrive in a growing economy and suffer in a stagnating one.* The fact has been empirically established by researchers by taking particular measures of firm performance. For instance, Mitra et. al. (2023) applied a time series panel data technique to study the impact of GDP growth rate on firm performance in India. The performance of 673 Indian manufacturing firms over the 18-year period from 2004–05 to 2021–22 was studied. Three different measures of business performance were considered. These were (1) return on assets, (2) return on equity and (3) a measure known as "Tobin's Q". All the three measures yielded the same conclusion viz. that the effect of GDP growth rate on the business performance of firms in India in the said period was *positive.* Performance improved when the growth rate of the economy increased and worsened when the growth rate fell. The paper also contains a survey of research in this area by other authors from which it is seen that similar results hold for some of the advanced economies as well as for the BRICS countries other than India and for firms in sectors other than manufacturing (for instance, for banks and financial service providers). (BRICS is an acronym for Brazil, Russia, India, China and South Africa).

The chain of arguments is now complete. Myopic business decision-making increases inequality. This has an adverse effect on the long-run growth of the economy. which, in turn, has an adverse effect on the performance of business firms. Thus, a single-minded pursuit of short-run profits hurts the business firms themselves in the long run.

4.3.4 Business firms' concern: Profits, not the share of profits in GDP

Is there a contradiction here with the fact, noted before, that, *at any given point of time* wages and profits are inversely related (so that if firms pay higher wages in order to increase labour productivity, their profits would fall)? Not really. The argument here is that in a growing economy, it is possible for firms to share the fruits of growth with the labourers in such a way that, *over time*, the (normal) profits of the firms increase and so do real wages.

Moreover, by letting the real wage rate grow at the same rate as the average productivity of labour, it is possible to prevent a fall in the labourers' share in GDP and, thus, to prevent a rise in the degree of inequality of income distribution and to free the growth path of the economy from the long-run constraint of inequality. Needless to say, this would prevent a rise in the share of GDP going to the profit-earners. Would the business firms consider this to be inimical to their interests? There are reasons to believe that the answer is in the negative. Any economic unit, whether it is a business firm or an individual, is concerned with its income, not with its *share* in the total income of the country. Thus, a business firm is hardly ever concerned with the *share* of business profits in GDP. It is concerned with the maximisation of its profits. The objective of maximising profits is better served if business decision-makers take a long-run view of profits.

4.4 Conclusion

While Chapter 3 described how inequality holds back economic growth, the present chapter has begun the discussion of the role that business decision-makers can play in enabling the economy to break out of this constraint. This chapter has been confined to the case of an economy that is supply-constrained (rather than demand-constrained). In such an economy, the tasks of maintaining and increasing factor productivities assume great urgency from the viewpoint of growth. The central message of the chapter is that prudent business decision-making that seeks to maximise long-run (rather than short run) profits of the firms can play a positive role in this context. Of particular importance are the matters of labour productivity and the wage policy of the business firms. Myopic behaviour aimed at holding real wages below the average productivity of labour may increase instantaneous profits but would hurt the long-run interests of the firms themselves since this would increase inequality (thereby restricting economic growth) and since the long-run profitability of business enterprises is intimately related to the long-run growth rate of the economy.

Notes

1 Uncertainties can be allowed if it is assumed that all uncertainties are *insurable* and that, like all other markets, the insurance market is also perfectly competitive.
2 The First Theorem of Welfare Economics is so called because there is a Second Theorem of Welfare Economics. In any economy, each individual starts with a given initial endowment of goods and services. The particular general equilibrium that the forces of perfect competition will take us to will depend on these initial endowments. Thus, the general equilibrium is not unique. Now, each general equilibrium leads to a Pareto-optimal distribution of utilities among the individuals. Thus, a Pareto-optimal distribution of utilities is also not unique. The Second Theorem of Welfare Economics says that any *given* Pareto-optimal distribution of utilities can be reached (through perfect competition) provided that the initial distribution of endowments is "right". In other words, for any pre-specified Pareto-optimal situation, there exists

some specification of endowments such that if these are the initial endowments, then the forces of perfect competition will lead to the particular general equilibrium that results in the particular Pareto-optimal distribution of utilities that was desired at the outset.

3 It is easily seen that this is *necessary* for profit maximisation. If price exceeds MC, the firm can increase profits by increasing the output by one unit because its revenue would increase more than its costs would. Thus, the initial output level was *not* profit maximising. Similarly, if price is less than MC, the firm made a loss on the last unit of output that it produced and a reduction in the output level is advisable. Maximum profits have not been achieved as long as price has not been equated to MC.

4 Production also requires intermediate inputs. However, these inputs are themselves outputs of other firms. Therefore, from the point of view of the economy as a whole, it is the constraints on the factors of production that are of importance in a supply-constrained economy.

5 It may seem that the *marginal* productivity of a factor (which means the change in output when the amount of the factor in question changes by a small amount and the amounts of all other factors are kept *unchanged*) would be a better measure of the factor's contribution in this respect. Actually, however, this does not solve the problem. For the reader who is familiar with the notion of a production function (which is a function with output as the dependent variable and the factors of production as the independent variables), it suffices to note that marginal productivity of a factor is the first *partial* derivative of the function with respect to the factor. Now, given any function, its first partial derivative (as well as all higher-order partial derivatives) with respect to any of the independent variables will, in general, also be a function of *all* the independent variables. For instance, if y is a function of, say, x and z, the first partial derivative of the function with respect to, say, x is, in general, itself a function of both x and z rather than one of x alone. Thus, it is not only the average but also the marginal productivity of a factor that is dependent on the amounts of *all* the factors.

6 For simplicity, ignore the fact that deforestation can add to the quantity of arable land. Deforestation will have undesirable consequences of its own.

7 There are various measures of the price level. For the purpose of calculating real wages, it is customary to use the Consumer Price Index. For obvious reasons, the workers' real standard of living depends on the prices of consumer goods and services rather than those of other commodities.

8 Consider the simple case where labour is the only factor of production. Let the production function of a firm be f. Thus, $y = f(l)$ where y is output and l is labour employed. Under perfect competition, the firm takes the output price (p, say) and the money wage rate (w, say) as given. Profit then is $pf(l) - wl$. Since p and w are treated as given, this is a function of l. If profit is to be maximised, it is necessary that l is such

that the first derivative of this expression is zero. Thus, $p(df/dl) - w = 0$. Hence, $df/dl = w/p$. However, df/dl, the first derivative of f with respect to l, is the marginal productivity of labour and w/p is the real wage rate. Moreover, the average productivity of labour y/l must equal df/dl. If $f/l < df/dl = w/p$, then $pf < wl$, that is, the value of output is less than the total wages of the workers. The firm would make a loss. If $f/l > w/p$, the firm would be making a profit. This would, however, attract other firms into the industry and the increased competition would push down the output price or push up the wage rate by increasing the demand for labour in the market. f/l would, thus, be brought to equality with w/p. Very similar remarks apply to the case where labour is *not* the only factor of production. All we have to do in this case is to note that the marginal productivity of any factor would be the first *partial* derivative of the production function with respect to the factor. It would, again, be a *necessary* condition for profit maximisation that the real rate of remuneration for each factor equals its marginal productivity.

References

Banerjee, A.K. (2023): *Economic Slowdown in India: An Introductory Analysis*, Routledge, New Delhi.

Bliss, C. and Stern, N. (1978): "Productivity wages and nutrition", *Journal of Development Economics*, Vol. 5, 331–398.

Dasgupta, P. and Roy, D. (1986): "Inequality as a determinant of malnutrition and unemployment: Theory". *Economic Journal*, Vol. 95, 1011–1034.

Dasgupta, P. and Roy, D. (1987): "Inequality as a determinant of malnutrition and unemployment: Policy". *Economic Journal*, Vol. 96, 177–188.

Dreze, J. (2023): "Wages are the worry, not just unemployment", *The Indian Express*, 13 April.

Goyal, A. (ed.) (2019): *A Concise Handbook of the Indian Economy in the 21st Century*. Oxford University Press, New Delhi.

Kapila, U. (ed.) (2020): *Indian Economy: The Great Slowdown?*, Academic Foundation, New Delhi.

Mitra, G., Gupta, V. and Gupta, G. (2023): "Impact of macroeconomic factors on firm performance: Empirical evidence from India", *Investment Management and Financial Innovations*, Vol. 20, 1–12.

Petridis, R. (1996): "Brassey's Law and the economy of high ages in nineteenth-century economics", *History of Political Economy*, Vol. 28, 583–606.

Saraswati, B. (2019): "Economic reforms and market competition in India: An assessment", Working Paper No. 216, Institute for Studies in Industrial Development, New Delhi.

Sasmal, J. (2016): *Resources, Technology, and Sustainability: An Analytical Perspective on Indian Agriculture*, Springer, New Delhi.

Sedai, A.K. (2016): "Competition or concentration: Analogy or chronology? A study of Indian Manufacturing sector post-New-Economic-Policy (1999–2013)", *Arthashastra*, Vol. 5, 35 – 47.

Smith, A. (1776): *An Inquiry into the Nature and Causes of the Wealth of Nations*, Vol. 1, W. Strahan, London.

Smith, A. (1778): *An Inquiry into the Nature and Causes of the Wealth of Nations*, Vol. 2, W. Strahan, London.

Solow, R.M. (1957): "Technical change and the aggregate production function", *Review of Economics and Statistics*, Vol. 39, 312–320.

van Briesbroeck, J. (2015): "How tight is the link between wages and productivity? A survey of the literature", Working Paper, ILO, Geneva.

www.ceicdata.com/en/indicator/india/labour-productivity-growth last accessed on July 3, 2023.

5 Individual rationality versus group rationality

5.1 Introduction

Chapter 4 discussed one reason why a single-minded pursuit of maximisation of short-run profits may turn out to be self-defeating. There is also a second reason that has nothing (or, at least, not that much) to do with the short-run-versus-long-run issue. Rather, it arises from the fact that what is rational from the viewpoint of each single decision-maker taken in isolation is not necessarily rational from the viewpoint of the group of decision-makers as a whole if the outcome depends on the decisions of all members of the group. Thus, while each single business manager may think that he or she is doing the right thing by trying to maximise instantaneous profits, this may actually hurt the interests of the private business sector of the economy, not only in the long run but also in the short. The present chapter is devoted to a discussion of the reasons why and how this opposition between individual rationality and group rationality arises in the context of business decision-making. We distinguish between the cases (i) where there are only a few large producers dominating the market and (ii) where there are a large number of independent producers. We shall discuss case (i) in detail in Section 5.2 and show that in this case there arises an apparent paradox that is known in game theory as the Prisoner's Dilemma. In Section 5.3, we shall remark briefly on case (ii). In both cases, such a dilemma for a business manager is seen to be particularly likely to arise if the economy in question is a demand-constrained one. There is, again, a vicious circle here. To an individual business manager, it seems that cutting down on labour costs by such means as outsourcing a large part of the total workload in the firm or taking advantage of digitisation to minimise the wage bill would be good for profit maximisation. In an economy that is demand-constrained to start with, however, this will make matters worse since in such an economy the main constraint on the profits and the expansion possibilities of the business sector comes from the deficiency of aggregate demand in the market. It is the workers that constitute the major source of demand for the produced goods. A reduction in the share of

DOI: 10.4324/9781032707082-5

workers in the national income will, therefore, depress demand even further. From the viewpoint of business managers, the important point here is that this would be a drag not only on the GDP of the country but also on the total profits of the business sector. The problem can be avoided, however, if business decision-making at the level of each individual firm takes cognisance of its effects on the business sector as a whole. Section 5.4 concludes the chapter.

5.2 A demand-constrained economy with a few large producers: Prisoner's Dilemma

5.2.1 The Prisoner's Dilemma game

There is a famous example used in game theory for the purpose of illustrating how there may arise a contradiction between individual rationality and group rationality. A *game* is an activity in which there are two or more participants ("players"). Each player has a choice among a number of strategies (or actions) that they can adopt. The outcome of the game is decided when each player has chosen a particular strategy. There are different possible outcomes corresponding to different strategic choices of the players. Each player has his or her own preferences over the different outcomes and chooses his or her strategy in accordance with these preferences.

The particular illustrative example of a game that will be used here for the present purposes is called the Prisoner's Dilemma. One version of the story behind the example goes as follows. A police officer has arrested two persons, X and Y, on the suspicion that the two had joined hands in committing two different crimes. One of the crimes is a fairly serious one and carries a heavy punishment under the law while the other is a relatively minor one with a lighter punishment. The officer does not have the required evidence to press charges against the two prisoners in the court for the *major* crime. Hence, conviction for that offence would be possible only if *at least one* of them confesses to the charge. There is, however, sufficient evidence of their involvement in the *minor* crime. Now, the officer calls the two prisoners separately and puts the following proposal to each of them. If neither prisoner confesses, then the officer cannot prove the major charge. In that case, the minor charge would be pressed, and both the prisoners would get light sentences. If both prisoners confess to the major crime, then the minor charge would not be pressed, and they would be convicted for the major crime but in that case the officer would plead with the judge that *medium* (rather than heavy) punishment be given to both the prisoners in view of the fact that their offence could not have been proved without their confession. However, if only *one* of the prisoners confesses while the other one does not (in which case, too, the major offence can be proved), then, again, the officer would not press charges for the minor crime but would ask for *heavy* punishment for the major crime as prescribed under the law for the prisoner who does not confess. He would, however, request the judge to set the *confessor* free on the ground that the case could not have been solved without his help.

Now, the question is: what would the prisoners do? Both X and Y have a choice between two strategies: confessing (C) and not confessing (NC). The important point here is that the outcome of the game depends on the strategic choices of *both* X and Y. It is realistic to assume that, for each of the two players, instant freedom, that is zero punishment, is the most preferred outcome followed by light, medium and heavy punishments, in decreasing order of preference. The possible outcomes of the game from the viewpoints of the two prisoners are summarised in Table 5.1.

The outcome of the game for any particular pair of strategy choices of the players is displayed in Table 5.1 in the form of a pair of words separated by a comma and written within parenthesis. The first word of the pair is the punishment received by X while the second is the punishment of Y. For instance, the entry (medium, medium) says that if X chooses to confess (i.e. if he chooses C) and so does Y, then the outcome of the game is that both get medium punishments. The entry (zero, heavy) shows that if X chooses C but Y chooses NC (i.e. if X confesses but Y does not), then X gets zero punishment but heavy punishment is given to Y and so on.

Now, what will be the actual outcome of the game, that is, what will be the strategy choices of the players? Start with the player X. X does not know what strategy will be chosen by Y. But X notices that if Y chooses C, then X's own optimal response is C which will then result in the outcome (medium, medium) and X will get medium punishment. The alternative for X is to choose NC. But then the outcome will be (heavy, zero), that is, X will get heavy punishment. Since medium is preferred to heavy, C would be a better strategy choice. X, of course, is not sure that Y will choose C. So he also ponders over the question what happens if Y chooses NC. It turns out that C will still be X's optimal strategy because that will result in the outcome (zero, heavy) and, hence, X will get zero punishment. The alternative of choosing NC will result in (light, light), that is, X would get light punishment which is worse than zero punishment. Thus, *whatever*

Table 5.1 Prisoner's Dilemma: Punishments of the prisoners for different strategic choices

X's strategy	Y's strategy	
	C	NC
C	(medium, medium)	(zero, heavy)
NC	(heavy, zero)	(light, light)

Note: C = Confessing; NC = Not confessing.

strategy is chosen by Y, X's optimal strategy is C. (In the language of game theory, C is X's *dominant* strategy).

What is interesting is that precisely the same is true of Y's strategic choice. Y does not know what X will do. But he will note that if X chooses C, then his own best choice is C since the outcome is then (medium, medium), that is, Y will get "medium" while the alternative of choosing NC will bring the outcome (zero, heavy), meaning that Y would then get "heavy" which would be worse for him. On the other hand, if X chooses NC, then also the optimal strategy for Y will be C because that will imply the outcome (heavy, zero), that is, he will then get zero punishment while the alternative of choosing NC will result in the outcome (light, light), that is, he will then get a light punishment. Thus, for Y also, C is the dominant strategy.

The result of the game is now obvious: both players will choose C and the outcome of the game is (medium, medium). Thus, both players end up getting medium punishment. Note that the players have ended up in this situation by pursuing their self-interests. Each player has chosen the strategy that is optimal from his or her own point of view. In this sense, each player has been individually rational.

Now comes the punchline of the story. To those who have no prior familiarity with the game of Prisoner's Dilemma, it comes as a big surprise. Look again at Table 5.1 and recall that the players can freely choose their strategies. Hence, there is nothing that prevents them from choosing NC. If both X and Y choose this strategy, then the outcome would be (light, light) and each of them (and, therefore, the group consisting of the two prisoners) would be better off than under the outcome (medium, medium). Apparently, by pursuing their self-interests, the players have actually ended up hurting their own interests!

Clearly, it is the absence of a cooperative attitude among the players that is the cause of the problem. If each prisoner decides to cooperate (among themselves, not with the police officer) by choosing the strategy NC, then the outcome that is optimal for the group as a whole is achievable. This type of behaviour, however, requires mutual *trust* among the players. When X chooses NC, X must be confident that Y also would choose NC and vice versa. If such trust is missing, the group-optimal is not achievable. Note that if X chooses NC, the best response of Y (from the viewpoint of Y's own interests) is not NC! Rather, it is C. X knows this. That is why X will refrain from choosing NC unless there is an overall framework of mutual trust and cooperation. The same, of course, is the situation from the viewpoint of Y.

The standard story of the Prisoner's Dilemma assumes only two players (viz. the two prisoners). It is easy to see, however, that the exact number of players is immaterial. The same conflict between individual rationality and group rationality would arise if there are three or more players. The crucial part of the story is that the police officer would be able to press charges against *all* the players for the major crime whenever there is even *one* player who confesses to it. This is what gives *each* player a strategic power to influence the outcome of the game and, unless the players are guided by group rationality, leads each of them to confess since that would be in line with his or her *individual rationality*. For further discussion about the game of Prisoner's Dilemma, see the classic game theory textbook by Luce and Raiffa (1957). Poundstone (1992) is a good introductory book addressed to the general reader and devoted exclusively to the Prisoner's Dilemma. More recent introductions to game theory that discuss this game include Gibbons (2018) and Osborne (2012).[1]

5.2.2   *Outsourcing and the fissured labour market*

What does the Prisoner's Dilemma have to do with the problems of business decision-making in an economy locked in the vicious circle of high inequality and slow growth? It is to this question that we now turn. Chapter 4 discussed why, in a supply-constrained economy, it is important for business managers to be aware of the long-run links between inequality and economic growth working through the channel of productivity. Consider now a demand-constrained economy. The rest of this section (Section 5.2), however, confines itself to the case of markets where there are only a few large producers. (The case of a market with a large number of producers will be discussed briefly in Section 5.3).

In a demand-constrained economy with a few large producers, business managers need to be aware of the importance of *factor remuneration policies* for the profit possibilities of the private business sector of the economy even in the short run. Arguments based on the Prisoner's Dilemma can be used to show that if each firm's manager is concerned exclusively with the profits of the particular firm managed by him or her, this will hurt the interests of the *group* of all business firms, that is, those of the business *sector* as a whole.

In discussing the factor remuneration policies of the firms, however, attention will be focused on their *wages and employment policies*. There are good reasons for this. In any economy, it is the workers (i.e. those who supply the factor of production *labour*) that constitute the majority of the factor suppliers and, indeed, the overwhelming majority of the population of the country. Therefore, when the produced output goes to the market for sale, it is the workers who become the major source of demand. Obviously, it is their wages that determine their purchasing power. Since the economy is assumed to be demand-constrained, the importance of increasing the purchasing power of the buyers should be obvious too. To show the relevance of the Prisoner's dilemma in this context, however, it is necessary to discuss, in a little detail, some of the developments that have recently taken place in the labour markets in most of the countries of the world including India.

Start by noting that, from the viewpoint of the manager of a particular firm, there is always a clear incentive to try to economise on labour costs. Until very recently, in the typical large business firm, the wage bill (i.e. wage rate multiplied by the number of workers) used to constitute one of the most important cost items. (There was a rule of thumb that said that approximately two-thirds of the total cost of production in such a firm were accounted for by the wage bill). A reduction in the wage bill was, therefore, considered to be conducive to profit maximisation. In practice, however, various factors prevented sharp reductions in the wage bill. In some cases, this was due to enlightened behaviour on the part of the firms. As explained in Chapter 4, high wages are often observed to increase labour productivity. Some employers did display awareness of this fact. More often, however, this was due to institutional factors. The minimum-wage laws set a floor on the wage rate. More importantly, there were trade unions engaged in collective bargaining with the employers. Wage bill reduction by reducing either wage rates or employment was not an easy proposition in the presence of strong trade unions. What gave the trade unions their strength was the fact that labour was an essential factor of production since there was limited substitutability between capital and labour. Technological progress had not yet reached the stage where machines could substitute human labour to a large extent.

Over the recent few decades, however, reducing the wage bill as a means of boosting short-run profits (or, at least, of preventing them from falling) has become a more attractive as well as a more feasible proposition so far as the producers are concerned. The attractiveness of the proposition in the long run is, of course, obvious because the beneficial effects of high wages on labour productivity via the greater ability of the workers to invest in their health and skill formation take time to register their effects. That, by itself, however, is a short-run-versus-long-run issue that has been discussed more fully in Chapter 4. In the context of the present chapter, what is more to the point is the nature of *technological progress* that has taken place in recent decades. Virtually, all recent technological innovations have been *labour-saving* rather than capital-saving, that is, they have taken the form of the discovery of new ways of producing things that have *reduced* the amount of *labour* required to produce one unit of a commodity (while usually increasing the amount of *capital* required to do so). The IT revolution has been an important development in this context. Moreover, over time in most countries there has been a decline in the relative prices of capital goods (with respect to those of other goods). This has provided the *economic incentive* to substitute capital for labour.

Trade unions, needless to say, have always been opposed to employment cuts. However, while they were able to put up strong opposition to any proposal of throwing any *presently employed* worker out of job, they could do little to prevent the producers from whittling down the rate of *new recruitments. Over time*, therefore, as the currently employed workers retired, there was a gradual decline in the rate of employment in the large companies. The consequent fall in the number of members of trade unions was the main reason behind the erosion of the strength of trade unions. As a result, in almost all countries of the world including India, the role of collective bargaining in setting wage and employment levels in the private sector is today by far less significant than it was a few decades ago.

The decline of the bargaining powers of the trade unions has also had a cascading effect on the whole structure and working of the labour market. The nature of the contracts that the producers enter into with the workers has changed quite radically. Large parts of the workload in the large companies are now regularly *outsourced*, typically to firms of smaller sizes. In many cases, the firms to which the work is outsourced, in turn, give some parts of the work to firms that are even smaller in size. The final product, however, is still sold in the market under the brand name of the original company. Thus, it is still a case of an economy dominated by a small number of large producers. Outsourcing helps large producers to cut down on labour costs even if the workers receive the same wage rates *per hour* as before from their new employers. This is because it relieves the large firms of some of the other responsibilities that they had to bear for workers on their payroll (for instance, the provision of provident fund and medical facilities). Moreover, the workers do *not* even receive the same per-hour wages as before. Many of the business firms to which the work is outsourced engage workers on a part-time basis. These workers are seldom unionised. Also, being small in size, they usually fall outside the purview of the minimum wage regulations. On the other hand, workers' unions in large firms no longer have the bargaining strength to prevent the proliferation of the system of outsourcing or sub-contracting. So far as the Indian economy is concerned, the whole process has also been aided to a considerable extent by the process of economic liberalisation that began in the early 1990s and has been gaining strength ever since. Measures taken under this programme have given greater powers to employers to downsize the workforce for the purpose of achieving greater economic efficiency. The way in which efficiency is defined in this context, however, frequently relates to the maximisation of *instantaneous* profits.

The type of labour market that has come into existence under these new arrangements is called the *fissured labour market*. It was Weil (2014) who coined this term. It has now come to be widely used. The word "fissure" literally means a crack or a split, for instance, in some part of a human body or on the surface of the earth. In the context of a labour market, it is used to describe a situation where outsourcing takes place on a large scale and there are significant differences in wages and working conditions between firms. There are firms of relatively large sizes on the one hand and a vast network of small firms and individuals operating as subcontractors, freelancers and gig workers on the other. To quote Weil (2014, 42), a modern large business firm is like a "solar system with a lead firm at its center and smaller workplaces orbiting around it". The notion of a fissured labour market has similarities with that of a *dual* labour market consisting of a *formal* and an *informal* part. An obvious similarity is that just as informal sector wages are typically lower than wages in the formal sector, people working in firms that operate under subcontracting earn, on the average, less than those that remain on the payroll of the large firms. An important *difference*, however, is that a fissured labour market is *defined* to be the result of outsourcing or subcontracting by large firms. A large part of the low-wage informal labour market, however, has an independent existence and is not related to the formal part by subcontracting. On the other hand, an outsourcing arrangement need not always be informal. In many cases, there are formal contracts between a large firm and a smaller one though the contract does not specify the wages that the latter will pay to its own employees.

The fissured labour market is presently receiving a lot of attention from economists in view of its many special implications. As was seen in Chapter 4, the traditional model of a perfectly competitive labour market predicts that each firm pays its workers a real wage rate that equals the marginal productivity of labour. In the long run, the wage rate would also equal average productivity. This implies, among other things, that there cannot be much inter-firm variation in wage rate. The wage rate would be the same for the same job in different firms and in different industries. Specifically, this implies that there would not be much inequality of wages in the economy. Needless to say, this is not what is observed in practice. At one time, it was thought that this was due to the presence of trade unions. It was the unions that, by engaging in collective bargaining over the wage rate, prevented the competitive outcome. The precise wage rate paid by a firm depended on the bargaining power of the workers in the particular firm. Thus, the wage rate for the same job was often different in different firms. As was seen above, however, the rise of the fissured labour market has been made possible by the decline of union power. Trade unions no longer have the ability to prevent large firms from outsourcing. Yet, the observed wage rates diverge from what the competitive model would predict. There is high variance of inter-firm and inter-industry wages. Different employers pay different wage rates for the same job. Moreover, as a result of increasing proliferation of outsourcing, this variance is increasing over time. (See, for instance, Freeman (2014)).[2] This has resulted in an increase over time in the inequality in the distribution of wage income *within* the subcontracting sector. Since it is this sector that now accounts for the major part of aggregate employment, this has led to rising inequality in the distribution of *wage income* in the economy. In turn, since aggregate wage income is the dominant part of aggregate income, inequality of wage incomes is the dominant part of the overall inequality of income distribution in the economy. Overall inequality has, therefore, increased.

Apart from its effect on inequality, however, the fissured labour market has had a negative impact on the *levels* of the wage rate as well. It is not surprising that the rates of wage paid to workers under the subcontracting system would be lower than those that prevailed in the large firms in the heydays of collective bargaining. What is surprising is the observed fact that subcontract wages are even lower than what they would be in a perfectly competitive labour market. Apparently, the disappearance of strong trade unions has *not* led to the emergence of the forces of perfect competition. In the context of the USA, a review of the available evidence shows that wage rates under the subcontracting system are at least 20 per cent less than the level in a fully competitive market. (See U.S. Department of the Treasury (2022)). While such comparisons with the reference point of perfect competition are not easily available for other economies, there are estimates of decline in wages as a result of outsourcing. For instance, in a number of industries in Germany, this decline was found to be in the range of 10 to 15 per cent. (See Goldschmidt and Schmieder (2017)). Moreover, most economists believe that these findings are actually *under-estimates* of the negative effect of outsourcing on the standard of living of the workers because as workers are eased out of the large firms, they lose not only the benefit of higher wages but also many other types of benefits. Little empirical research, however, seems to have been done on the wage effects of outsourcing in the Indian context. It seems reasonable, however, to expect similar trends in the Indian labour market since the increasing dependence of large Indian firms on the practice of outsourcing is well-known.[3] On the matter of the effects of outsourcing on *productivity* in India, see, for instance, Kar and Dutta (2018).

5.2.3 *To outsource or not to outsource, that is the question*

Downsizing the wage bill and creating a fissured labour market by practising widespread outsourcing seems to be an attractive strategy for large firms. It helps them to be more efficient. In fact, outsourcing has come to be considered to be a major innovation so far as business strategy is concerned. Greater efficiency, of course, is a euphemism for greater profits but that by itself is not something that one can object to because profit maximisation is the objective of a business firm after all.[4] Recall, however, that in this chapter we are concerned with a demand-constrained economy. What constrains economic growth in such an economy (as opposed to that of a supply-constrained one) is not low labour productivity as such but inadequate demand for the produced goods in the market. In this context, a large firm is locked in a Prisoner's Dilemma while deciding whether or not to pursue a programme of cutting down on labour costs by downsizing its workforce by such means as outsourcing. The basic idea is, again, quite simple. The savings in wage costs and the greater degree of efficiency that is achieved thereby make outsourcing an optimal strategy from the point of view of each single large firm. *All* large firms would, therefore, tend to follow this strategy if each of them is concerned exclusively with its own profits. As we have discussed above, however, when outsourcing is practised by all large firms, the labour market is fissured. There is a fall in the *average* wages as well as an increase in the degree of *inequality* in the income distribution in the economy as a whole. Both of these have negative impacts on aggregate demand. If there was already a demand deficiency problem to begin with, the situation, rather than improving, would actually get worse. The increase in efficiency achieved by outsourcing is of no avail since there is insufficient demand for the produced output and the profit possibilities are not actually realised.[5]

Consider an industry with only two identical and large firms, X and Y, producing the same commodity. Since there are a small number, just two, of large firms, each firm is a large part of the whole industry, and its unilateral action will significantly impact the whole industry. There is demand deficiency, preventing the firms from making profits. Assume that the firms wish to do something about the problem (rather than just ignoring it). There are two different (and exactly opposite) strategies that a firm can adopt: (1) decrease the wage bill to bolster profits and (2) increase the wage bill, that is, pay higher wages in the hope that this would increase people's purchasing power and, therefore, boost demand. Call these strategies DEC and INC, respectively.

What will actually happen to the profits of a firm when a firm adopts a particular strategy depends on which strategy the other firm adopts. Now, if both firms adopt DEC, then aggregate demand will fall. This will hurt both firms. However, both firms have also cut labour costs. This protects their profits to some extent. Assume that the net result is that each firm ends up earning a small (though positive) amount of profit (say, S). (Positivity is an inconsequential assumption. None of the conclusions that we shall reach below will change if S is zero or even negative).

What happens if X adopts DEC and Y adopts INC? This would be the best possible situation for X. Since one firm increases the wage bill and the other firm reduces it, we may assume that aggregate demand in the market remains more or less the same. However, X has cut down on labour costs. Moreover, since this may enable X to *reduce* the price of the commodity, X can lure some customers away from Y, thus increasing its own *market share*. This is an additional benefit for X from the demand side, quite apart from the benefit obtained from cost reduction. Assume that this double benefit results in an amount of profit (L, say) for X which is considerably larger than S. Y would face the opposite prospect. The increase in wage bill increases its costs, exerting a downward pressure on profits. Moreover, since X can afford to cut price but Y cannot (since its costs have, in fact, increased), it will lose customers to firm X. Assume that this double jeopardy results in a very small (VS) amount of profit for Y. Specifically, assume that VS < S. Symmetrically, assume that if X adopts strategy INC and Y adopts DEC, then the outcome is VS for X and L for Y.

There remains the case where both X and Y adopt the strategy INC. In this case, both firms increase wages and it seems reasonable to assume that the increase in the consumers' purchasing power leads to a large increase in aggregate demand and boosts profits (despite the cost increase) for both the firms. Moreover, this favourable demand effect may be assumed to be larger in magnitude than in the cases where only one of the two firms raises wages. Note that price competition in this case would be of no avail since the firms are identically placed with respect to both demand and costs. On balance, it can be assumed that in this case, the amounts of profits of the two firms would be the same (M, say) and that M would be smaller than L but larger than S. We, therefore, have: VS < S < M < L. (The symbols VS, S, M and L have been chosen to stand for "very small", "small", "medium" and "large", respectively).

Table 5.2 displays the profit outcomes for the two producers for the different combinations of wage policies.

The profit outcomes for the two producers for any particular pair of strategy choices have been displayed in the table in the form of a pair of symbols separated by a comma and written within parentheses. The first member of the pair is the amount of profit earned by X while the second is the amount earned by Y. For instance, the entry (S, S) says that if both X and Y adopt the strategy DEC, then each of them earns a small amount of profit (S); the entry (L, VS) says that if X chooses DEC but Y chooses INC, then X earns a large amount (L) of profit while the amount earned by Y is very small viz. VS; and so on.

Table 5.2 A game of Prisoner's Dilemma between two large producers

X's strategy	Y's strategy	
	DEC	INC
DEC	(S, S)	(L, VS)
INC	(VS, L)	(M, M)

Note: DEC = Decreasing the wage bill; INC = Increasing the wage bill; VS, S, M and L denote very small, small, medium and large profits, respectively; VS < S < M < L.

Assume that each producer prefers a larger amount of profit to a smaller one. Then one has only to look back at Table 5.1 to convince ourselves that Table 5.2 describes a Prisoner's Dilemma. For each producer, DEC is the dominant strategy. Hence, if X and Y are guided by their narrow self-interests, then the result of the game is that both choose DEC. But, by doing so, they actually behave irrationally because each of them could have easily chosen the strategy INC, guaranteeing an amount of profit M which is greater than S. Again, the same result would hold if the number of producers was greater than two but small enough to ensure that each producer is a significant part of the whole industry. Thus, if an economy is demand constrained and is dominated by a handful of large producers, then even in the short run, there may arise a conflict between each producer's narrow self-interest and the interest of the group consisting of all the producers.

5.3 Demand-constrained economy with a large number of independent firms

This short section discusses the case of a demand-constrained economy with a large number of independent firms. We can afford to be brief because while the problem of divergence between individual rationality and group rationality reappears here, the reason for this divergence is more easily seen in this context. No game theoretic analysis is necessary. Since there are a large number of firms, each single firm is an insignificant part of the whole group of such firms and also of the economy as a whole. In particular, such a firm, acting singly, cannot boost aggregate demand in the economy to any significant extent by expanding employment or paying high wages even if it wishes to. Moreover, each such firm has to take all market prices (including the price of the good that it produces) as given. It cannot influence them by any unilateral action. Thus, there is no question of luring customers away from other firms by lowering the product price. In the presence of the demand constraint, therefore, the only feasible way for the firm to improve profitability (or cut losses) is to scale down production and reduce the wage bill (and other costs). However, all input prices (including the wage rate) are exogenously given and cannot be influenced by the firm. Hence, the firm's only recourse is to reduce employment. Note that this will not have any significant impact on *aggregate* employment in the economy.

However, while this is the rational thing to do for the firm, the problem is that this would be the rational thing to do for *each* of all the other firms if all firms are alike. Hence, if each firm is guided by its own interest, *all* firms will cut back employment and *that* will have a *significant* negative impact on aggregate employment and wage bill. This will reduce aggregate demand in the economy *immediately* (rather than only in the long run). Since there was a demand deficiency problem to begin with, this will make matters worse for all firms. What is called for is a rise in aggregate demand. Thus, again, what is rational for each individual firm is not rational for the business sector of the economy as a whole.

5.4 Conclusion

To summarise, this chapter has been concerned with some of the problems that business decision-makers face in an economy that is demand-constrained. From their respective points of view, it is perfectly rational for each producer to try to bypass the problem of inadequacy of demand for the produced goods in the market by cutting down on labour costs in order to maintain profitability. In the case where the market is dominated by a handful of large producers (so that each producer is a significant part of the market), it is no wonder this leads each producer to take recourse to widespread outsourcing, thus giving rise to the so-called fissured labour market. This is a major current trend in most of the countries of the world including India. This type of policy, however, is seen to be irrational from the viewpoint of the whole private business sector of the economy. It does not solve the demand problem faced by the business sector. On the contrary, it actually exacerbates the problem. Interestingly enough, similar remarks apply also to the case where there are a large number of producers none of whom is large enough to be able to influence aggregate supply and demand by its unilateral action. In both cases, the basic problem is that, given any group of decision-makers, what is the rational thing to do from the viewpoint of each member of the group may turn out to be irrational from that of the group as a whole. It is possible, however, for business decision-makers to help the economy in finding a solution to the demand problem (and to help themselves in the process) by following policies that are rational from the viewpoint of the group of all business firms.

Notes

1 While this is not a book about game theory, the curious reader may note that the Prisoner's Dilemma game was first designed in 1950 by Melvin Dresher and Merrill Flood, two scientists working at the Rand Corporation. It received its name from the Princeton mathematician Albert Tucker. Luce and Raiffa (1957) was the first book to discuss it.
2 It is the large and increasing inter-firm wage differences for the same jobs even in the absence of labour market imperfections caused by trade unions that economists have not been able to explain fully up to now. This is a topic of cutting-edge research. Freeman (2014) reports that he had asked the legendary Chicago economist Gary Becker a few months before the latter's death what a possible explanation of this

riddle could be. Becker's reply was that it was a hard problem. He advised Freeman to keep working on it. For the purposes of this book, however, finding an explanation of the wage differences is not particularly important.

3 As is well-known, in the 1990s and the 2000s, there was *offshoring* of workloads by large producers in the USA and other countries. While this, too, is a form of outsourcing, the discussion in the text is primarily concerned here with the effects of *domestic* outsourcing by large firms.

4 It can be argued that when large firms become more efficient, they can afford to pass on some of the benefits to consumers by lowering the prices of their products. If they do so, then the net effect of outsourcing on the economic well-being of the workers that cease to be on the payrolls of these firms becomes ambiguous in theory. Their wages and working conditions worsen but they gain as consumers in the market for the produced goods. However, there does not seem to be any statistical evidence to reject the hypothesis that they lose on balance.

5 There is an apocryphal story which is worth retelling here. Henry Ford II, grandson of Henry Ford, the legendary entrepreneur and founder of Ford Motors, was showing Walter Reuther, the leader of the powerful trade union United Automobile Workers, around a newly opened fully automated plant of Ford Motors. Ford laughingly asked Reuther, "Can you collect union dues from those robots?" Reuther retorted, "Can you sell Ford cars to them?" Reuther's point obviously was that while productivity could be vastly improved by using robots in place of human workers, in order to sell the produced cars in the market Ford would need to have human beings with the required purchasing power.

References

Freeman, R.B. (2014): "The subcontracted labor market: David Weil's book, "The Fissured Workplace", describes a disturbing trend for workers", *Perspectives on Work*, Vol. 18, 38–109.

Gibbons, R. (2018): *A Primer in Game Theory*, Pearson, New York.

Goldschmidt, D. and Schmieder, J.F. (2017): "The rise of domestic outsourcing and the evolution of the German wage structure", *Quarterly Journal of Economics*, Vol. 132, 1165–1217.

Kar, S. and Dutta, M. (2018): "Outsourcing and productivity during economic crisis: Evidence from Indian manufacturing firms", *Arthaniti: Journal of Economic Theory and Practice*, Vol. 17, 168–182.

Luce, R.D. and Raiffa, H. (1957): *Games and Decisions*, Wiley, New York.

Osborne, M.J. (2012): *An Introduction to Game Theory*, Oxford University Press, New York.

Poundstone, W. (1992): *Prisoner's Dilemma*, Doubleday, New York.

U.S. Department of the Treasury. (2022): *The State of Labor Market Competition*, Department of the Treasury, Wahington.

Weil, D. (2014): *The Fissured Workplace*, Harvard University Press, Cambridge, MA.

6 Epilogue

6.1 Introduction

This is the concluding chapter of the book. Its main purpose is to discuss the possible steps that can be taken to motivate business managers to take cognisance of the vicious circle of high inequality and slow economic growth. It may seem that this discussion would be superfluous since, as has already been shown in the preceding chapters, it is not only in the broader social interests but also in the interests of the business firms themselves that business decision-making should be concerned with the question how the economy can break out of this circle. However, as emphasised in the preceding chapters, in reality business firms very often tend to lose sight of this fact and, in the process, end up with decisions that are not only socially inoptimal but also inoptimal from the viewpoint of the private business sector of the economy. The *practical* task of making business managers aware of the *true* (rather than the apparent) interests of the private business sector is, therefore, non-trivial and merits a separate discussion.

Before coming to this main agenda, however, the chapter will briefly discuss two issues that have not been mentioned so far in this book but are likely to make the social impacts of business decision-making even more important in the coming years than they have been in the past. One of these is *global warming* and the other is the rise of *digital technology* in general and *artificial intelligence* in particular. Section 6.2 discusses these topics.

Section 6.3 discusses the role that government and the society at large can play in inducing business managers to take socially optimal decisions. It explains why governmental efforts to promote *corporate social responsibility* by mandating that the companies have to spend a specified percentage of their profits on social activities are unlikely to be of much avail.

The first of the two subsections of Section 6.4 suggests that a better course of action would be to overhaul the *management education* programmes and to try to make (the would-be as well as the practising)

DOI: 10.4324/9781032707082-6

business managers aware of the issues that have been discussed in the previous chapters. The second subsection is devoted to the discussion of a different type of social programme. This has to do with motivating the *investors*, that is, those who supply capital to the firms. A social movement exhorting investors to patronise those companies that desist from taking myopic decisions and seek to address the problem of economic inequality is already afoot in some countries. The experience so far has been encouraging. A similar experiment in the Indian context seems to be called for. It may seem that since the corporate sector in India is not directly responsible for more than a small percentage of the total output and employment of the Indian economy, this type of programmes would not have a large impact on the economy. However, the idea is that the investors would examine not only whether large companies desist from taking myopic decisions but also whether these companies demand the same prudence on the part of those other firms with which they have outsourcing arrangements.

Section 6.5 places the central concern of the book (viz. rational business decision-making) in the context of the recent debate over what has been called "woke capitalism". Section 6.6 concludes the chapter (and the book).

6.2 Two megathreats

6.2.1 Global warming

Nouriel Roubini, the economist who had predicted the Global Financial Crisis of 2007 long before it occurred, has more recently warned us about a number of threats that loom large on the horizon and that are very likely to put human civilisation to extreme stress in the coming years. (See Roubini (2022)). Two of these "megathreats" are related to the type of economic problems that we have been discussing in this book. These are the threats posed by (i) global warming and (ii) the rise of artificial intelligence (and, more generally, digital technology).

Consider the problem of global warming first. It has been predicted that in the course of the present century the average temperature of our planet is going to increase by at least 3 degrees Celsius over what it was just before the Industrial Revolution unless preventive steps are taken. Global warming is caused by the carbon emission that takes place in the process of production and consumption of goods. Production itself (i.e. the transformation of inputs into outputs) often emits greenhouse gases. The degradation of nature that accompanies the process of supplying inputs to the production process also contributes to the predicament. Deforestation (leading to climate change) and excessive extraction of natural resources are instances of such degradation. Sometimes the process of consumption also emits greenhouse gases. Driving an automobile is an example. Experts predict that even before the end of the twenty-first century, global warming will cause flooding of all coastal cities of the world and desertification of large tracts of land.

All this is apprehended to have disastrous consequences on economic growth. Many economists fear that in the course of the next 40 years, the growth rates of most of the economies of the world including India may fall significantly from their present levels. As we have seen (in Section 4.3.3), sluggish economic growth is bad news for business firms. It damages their profit prospects. At the same time, it increases inequality in the economy and tightens the noose of the vicious circle on the economy posed by the nexus between rising inequality and falling growth rate. Global warming is, therefore, a daunting prospect for the business firms as much as it is so for the public at large. That is what makes the problem worth mentioning in a book on business decision-making.

Global warming and the resulting environmental catastrophe can be avoided only if suitable preventive actions are taken. Since the problem is global, it is obvious that such actions need to be adopted at the global level. *All* producers in *all* countries must be induced to take appropriate measures, the most important of which is the development and adoption of new technologies that would avoid (or, at least, minimise) carbon emission. However, in this respect, the advanced countries have a special responsibility. It is only these countries that can afford the heavy expenditure on research and development that is initially required for the purpose. Moreover, at least in some cases, reducing carbon emission may require us to accept a lower rate of economic growth. That, however, would be an unacceptably high sacrifice for other countries where a significant percentage of the population still lives below the poverty line. It is only the people in the richer countries where material comforts of life have already reached a high level that can afford to abstain from demanding still higher levels of material consumption.[1]

Needless to say, a global policy framework that is needed in this context can only be based on international economic cooperation and understanding. Unfortunately, that seems a far cry at the moment. However, it is not the case that absolutely nothing can be done *unilaterally* by a developing economy. There are measures that can be taken at the country level and that will benefit the domestic economy significantly. Preventing deforestation, discouraging the use of plastic and other non-biodegradable materials and adopting environment-friendly technology are among the most important examples of such measures. In India, as in all other countries, a large part of the total annual carbon emission is accounted for by the production of energy. Recent research has shown that by choosing appropriate technologies in the energy sector, it is possible to ensure that the Indian economy is set on a growth path that would keep the total annual carbon emission in the country within sustainable limits. (See, for instance, Sengupta (2020)). Government policies (such as tax and subsidy measures) obviously have a very important role to play in this context. So far as business firms are concerned, the type of arguments that were used in Chapter 5 can again be invoked here to show that it is in the interests of the business sector as a whole to cooperate with the government in the implementation of these policies. Abstaining from doing so (for instance, by evading the taxes or by refraining from adopting the appropriate technologies) may be rational for each individual firm but will hurt the interests of the group consisting of all firms. We do not repeat those arguments here.

6.2.2 Artificial intelligence: The gig economy

6.2.2.1 Technological progress and labour displacement

Technological progress, by definition, means the invention of new techniques of production that increase productive efficiency (i.e. increase the amount of output that can be obtained from the same levels of employment of the factors of production). Historically, however, it is often seen to take the form of invention of new *machines* that can perform the work hitherto done by human labour much faster and much more accurately. Use of the machines, therefore, would permit the firm to reduce the use of labour. Output would increase and labour cost would decrease. Needless to say, however, the machines would involve investment. Whether a firm would actually decide to use a newly invented machine would depend on whether, on balance, it would be profitable to do so.

The machines that made the Industrial Revolution possible were obviously of the "profitable" type. The manifold increase in output and the substantial saving on wage costs that they brought with them not only increased profits but also lowered the average cost of production, thereby lowering the market prices of the goods or services. Thus, the consumers gained too. Moreover, the technological progress often brought into existence many new types of goods and services (or, at least, new variants of them). The consumers gained from this increased *diversity* of the consumables also.

But what would be the effect of labour-displacing technological progress on the level of *employment* in the economy? It may seem that employment of human labour would contract and there would be widespread unemployment and social conflict. Indeed, this happened within many firms in course of the Industrial Revolution, sometimes with tragic consequences. A well-known example is the case of Luddites who went about smashing knitting looms in the cotton and woollen mills of early-nineteenth-century England.[2] Millowner William Horsefall who had installed knitting machines in his plants and laid off workers was shot dead in 1812.

However, as is now well-known, the effect of Industrial Revolution on *aggregate* employment in the British economy was positive, rather than negative. The expanded profit opportunities led many new firms to enter the market. Because of the lower market prices, they enjoyed the patronage of the consumers. Thus, employment opportunities increased in the aggregate. Many of those who lost jobs in one firm or in one line of production were absorbed elsewhere, possibly after a time gap. While there were some who failed to find alternative employment and faced penury, many new entrants into the labour market were gainfully employed. On balance, there was an unmistakable expansion of aggregate employment, at least eventually, if not immediately.

Broadly, the employment effects of technological progress in other countries and in later times were similar up to around the 1980s. Things started changing with the arrival of the information technology (IT) revolution. In many cases, there was substitution of digital equipment for human labour. In some cases, however, the net effect of this on employment even within a firm was ambiguous because there was an opposition between negative and positive effects. For instance, the advent of automatic teller machines rendered conventional human tellers in banks superfluous but this also enabled banks to engage in aggressive branch expansion since the cost of doing so was now considerably lower. Moreover, it is not clear whether IT enabled enough new firms to enter the market to make the aggregate effect on employment unambiguously positive. Quite a lot depended on the rate of literacy and computer numeracy in the country, supply of electricity, etc. As result, there were considerable differences in the experiences of different countries or, in cases of large countries such as India, even in those of different regions within a country.

6.2.2.2 *Digital platforms: The gig economy*

At one stage of the IT revolution, it was mainly work done inside the office that was digitised. An office employee would be using calculators and computers for doing what had been previously done manually. In recent decades, however, IT has revolutionised *communication* technology. In particular, the invention of smartphones with mobile internet connectivity has profoundly affected the economy. One important instance of the economic impact of digital communication is seen in the labour market in the form of the *gig economy*. Since this new development has implications for inequality, the matter deserves some discussion here.

A gig economy is an economy where a large part of the labour force consists of the so-called "gig workers". This term was originally intended to mean short-term contractual workers and freelancers who were usually poorly paid. Of late, however, it has come to mean specifically the digital-platform-based workers. A gig economy is "an economic system that uses online platforms to digitally connect on-demand freelance workers with requesters (i.e. customers or clients) to perform fixed-term tasks" (Kuhn and Maleki (2017)). The digital platforms play a mediating role between the gig workers and the customers that they serve. Typical examples of gig workers are drivers employed by taxi-service platforms such as Uber and Ola and food deliverers employed by Swiggy, Zomato, etc. In most cases, what the digital platforms produce is *services* rather than physical goods. However, the owners of the digital platforms are themselves large companies rather than small "satellite" producers. Again, therefore, we are in the case where the economy is dominated by a few large producers.

Gig employment, however, is quite different from the conventional employment of either permanent or temporary workers by business firms. In fact, very often the platforms claim that the gig workers are not their employees but "partners" or "independent contractors". Accordingly, the payments the workers receive from the platforms are not even called wages or salaries but are given other names such as "incentives". In most cases, a gig worker fails to earn a decent income.

Like the fissured labour market discussed in Chapter 5, the gig economy is also a result of a general process of contraction in the rate of creation of jobs of the conventional type in the economy. This is the commonality between the two. In the absence of regular jobs with decent salaries, people are forced to accept gig work. There are, however, some differences with the fissured market as well. In particular, outsourcing by large companies does not play a direct role here. For instance, it is *not* the case that Uber or Swiggy has received an outsourcing contract from any company. Rather, gig employment is cited as an example how new technology can create *new types* of jobs in an economy. Nevertheless, for our purposes here, what is important is that it is the downsizing of large companies in other parts of the economy and the resulting fall in the rate of employment of the conventional type in the economy as a whole that are the root causes behind the emergence of the gig economy.

In recent years, the gig economy in India has grown at a fast pace. Estimates of its present and possible future sizes, however, vary widely. NITI Aayog (2022) reported that in 2020–21, there were 77 lakh (7.7 million) gig workers in the country and that the number was expected to swell to 2.35 crore (235 million) by 2029–30. According to BCG (2021), the number can shoot up to 9 crore (90 million) in due course. On the other hand, as per the India Brand Equity Foundation (IBEF), there are already over 1.5 crore (15 million) gig workers in the country and there will be as many as 35 crore (350 million) of them by as early as

2025 (see IBEF (2021)). For further discussion on India's gig economy, see, for instance, Pant and Majumdar (2022).

While the gig economy has certainly created new types of jobs, many experts are of the opinion that it has actually worsened the conditions of the working class as a whole. In India, while downsizing of firms has taken place in many segments of the private sector, the gig economy has created new jobs in just a handful of occupations (mainly, taxi-driving, home delivery of food or groceries and data entry). It is not clear whether, on balance, the gig economy has increased employment opportunities in the economy as a whole or has actually reduced it. The falling rate of new job creation in the country in recent years points towards the latter possibility.

Moreover, the working conditions of gig workers are deplorable. While comprehensive data on gig workers in India do not seem to be available, there is fragmentary evidence. Usually, due to their status as "partners" or "independent contractors" (rather than salaried employees), gig workers have very low base pay, with the major part of their earning coming from incentive payments. The rates of incentive are, however, so low that to make ends meet they have to spend long hours at work (between 12 and 15 hours every day). Moreover, they have to bear several other costs such as those associated with the purchase of essential equipment (for instance, a smartphone and a motorbike) and fuel. On top of all this, unlike company employees, they have no legal claim to medical or other social security benefits. (See, for instance, the report written by Sekharan (2022) for India Development Review, an independent media platform).

The picture is hardly any different in the advanced economies. In recent times, there have been some comprehensive statistical surveys in some of these countries. In a recent survey by the University of Bristol on the gig economy in Britain, more than half of the respondents reported that they earned less than the legal minimum wage of the country. The median respondent earned 8.97 British pounds per hour while the minimum wage was 9.50 pounds. Moreover, more than 75 per cent of the respondents reported that they were suffering from work-related insecurity and anxiety. See University of Bristol (2023). The US experience is broadly similar. See, for instance, Abraham et. al. (2018) and Duggan et. al. (2021).

Altogether, the labour market effect of the digital-technology-driven gig economy has been quite different from that of the technological progress of the previous centuries. Technological progress has always killed some jobs and created some others. In bygone times, however, it usually led to a net increase in employment opportunities in the economy as a whole (at least, after a time gap). Moreover, the new jobs were better paid than those that were eliminated.

Under these circumstances, it seems fair to infer that the emergence of the gig economy has led to a worsening of the overall economic condition of the class of people who previously had regular jobs but are now forced to take up gig jobs. On the other hand, there have been increases in the salaries and incentives of the fortunate few that are still in regular jobs in large companies. As a result, there has been an increase in the inequality of the distribution of *wage incomes*. As we have had occasion to remark before, inequality of wage income accounts for the major part of the overall inequality of income distribution in the economy. Thus, overall inequality has tended to increase. As we have been emphasising all along, this is bad portent for the economy as a whole as well as for the private business sector of the economy.

6.2.2.3 *Artificial intelligence*

The advent of artificial intelligence (AI) has brought yet another round of very significant change in the economic scenario. Although AI is only just beginning to make its presence felt, most economists are of the opinion that its impact on the labour market is going to be profound and truly disturbing. In particular, it is apprehended that the gig economy will become even more pervasive than it is now. Until recently, labour displacement due to the use of digital equipment such as computers or smartphones with internet connections took the form of speeding up of work by replacing "manpower" with "automated horsepower" or by making communications and information gathering easier. AI, however, is doing something that is completely unprecedented. It is replacing human "brainpower". It is leading to the development of computers that are *intelligent* in the sense that they are able to think. That is how this type of technology got its name.[3] The effect of AI on the labour market is, therefore, apprehended to be much more pervasive and deleterious than that of the type of technological progress that we were used to seeing until very recently. Not only employment in firms that work with backdated technologies but also aggregate employment in the economy would now decline. When machines become intelligent, no job of any kind is secure. Whatever a human worker (no matter how low-end or high-end in terms of salary) does, a machine would do better and faster.

The precise distribution of the employment effect over the different parts of the economy is, however, a matter over which economists are not yet in complete agreement. The National Science and Technology Council (NSTC) of the USA is of the opinion that AI would affect low-wage jobs most (see NSTC (2016)). The majority of experts, however, seem to believe that, on the contrary, it is low-wage jobs that would be relatively protected. It is the middle class, the so-called white-collar workers, that will have to bear the major part of the impact. It is skilled or intelligence-based work that would now be assigned to machines. This will lead to greater cost-saving for the firms. Moreover, it will not be profitable to use intelligent machines at a very small scale (for instance, for the purpose of doing the work performed by a single housemaid in one family or by one janitor or night guard in an office or residential building). There is now a real danger that the overwhelming majority of the workers in the economy would end up in low-end jobs. In other words, practically the entire work force would be in the gig economy.

The important point to note here is that economic inequality would increase, no matter whether both low- and high-wage employment decline (while profits of firms increase) or it is only high-wage employment that contracts. In the latter case, where relatively well-paid workers face economic extinction (or are reduced to low-wage ones), what would happen *additionally* is that *polarisation* would increase. Polarisation means the process under which the society gets split between a small number of groups of people where there is a high degree of homogeneity *within* each group and a high degree of heterogeneity *between* groups. Extreme polarisation takes place when the society is divided into just two groups of people: the very poor and the very rich.[4] Now, any increase in the degree of polarisation increases social disharmony and unrest. AI, therefore, is likely to erode the bedrock of social trust on which the smooth functioning of an economy vitally depends.

Thus, it is widely believed that the rise of AI would not only accentuate the already-existing problem of demand deficiency in the economy by increasing inequality but also create social unrest by increasing polarisation. Needless to say, all this implies that each firm would be tempted to use AI for the purpose of increasing profits. However, if all of them do so, then the interests of the business sector as a whole would be further jeopardised.

In the coming years, therefore, the task of sensitising business managers to the need for socially optimal business decision-making is likely to turn out to be even more urgent than it is at the moment.

6.3 Corporate social responsibility

What, if anything, can be done in practice to nudge business managers towards making decisions that would be optimal for both the society as a whole and the private business sector? The most obvious suggestion in this connection would be to emphasise what has been called "corporate social responsibility" (CSR). If this term is taken in its literal sense, then it is basically what the present book is all about. In this section, however, we discuss CSR as it is understood in the context of company law. It was certainly a laudable move on the part of the Government of India to incorporate the idea of CSR in the framework of law. In fact, India was the first country in the world to do so. In April 2014, CSR was made mandatory for companies in India by means of an amendment of the Companies Act, 2013. Currently, every company with a net worth of at least Rs. 500 crore (5 billion) or an annual turnover of at least Rs. 1000 crore (10 billion) or a net annual profit of at least Rs. 5 crore (50 million) is required to spend at least 2 per cent of the average of its annual profit in the previous three years on projects of a social nature such as promoting education, gender equality, environmental sustainability, eradication of hunger and poverty etc. Subsequently, a number of other countries (such as China, Indonesia, the UK and South Africa) have followed the example of India.

The general spirit of the CSR-related legislations is in line with that of this book. However, as argued in the previous chapters, if the economy of the country is to be brought out of the vicious circle of high inequality and slow growth, it is necessary to induce the business firms to follow appropriate wage and employment policies. The focus of this argument is on the *economic* aspects of business decisions. To be sure, business expenditure on the social projects would bring some indirect economic benefits also. What is needed, however, is an emphasis on the main economic issue. It is easy to see that, requiring a firm to spend a *specified* proportion of its net profit on a social issue will not have any impact on its *economic* decisions (for instance, on the level of output that it decides to produce or the amounts of labour and other factors of production that it decides to employ).[5] Thus, CSR legislations do not touch the main issues that were discussed in the two preceding chapters.[6] Such legislative actions do prod business firms to engage in charities and do deserve appreciation. The basic issue that this book is concerned with, however, relates to the economic interests of the country in general and of the business sector in particular rather than to matters of philanthropy.

6.4 Public actions to motivate optimal business decision-making

6.4.1 Management education

While CSR-oriented legislative actions are unlikely to be of much relevance for the type of problems that this book is concerned with, this should not be taken to imply that there is no role that the society at large can play in this context. On the contrary, public action, possibly with some support from the government and other agencies, is likely to be able to play a very important role. "Public action" here essentially means action by members of the public. This will include actions of individuals, groups or associations of individuals, governments, international agencies, educational institutions and all types of non-government organisations.

One of the most obvious of types of public action that can motivate managers to adopt decisions that would be optimal from the viewpoint of the economy as a whole as well as from that of the business firms is to give an appropriate orientation to *management education*.

The received wisdom passed on to generations of students in business management courses is centred on Milton Friedman's now-famous 1970 interview given to the *New York Times Magazine* which espoused the view that the only social responsibility of business is to "increase its profits". This was also the basis of the "agency theory" put forward by Jensen and Meckling (1976). The idea was that so far as a public limited company was concerned, it was the shareholders who were the "principals". The professional managers were the "agents" whose main task was to look after the interests of the principals by maximising shareholder returns. This was the intellectual foundation of the shareholders' movement that began in the USA in the 1980s. The objective of the movement was to restrain the managers from pursuing any other aim. It was demanded that managers' pay and other incentives were to be based solely on shareholder returns. For a long time since then, this was also the basic theme around which all management education courses were woven.

However, it was also this way of looking at management science that led over time to downsizing of the labour force by outsourcing and other means. At the present point of time, it is obvious that a would-be manager of a business firm needs to be made aware of the fact that while profit maximisation is the legitimate objective of any business firm, it is often very important to resist the temptation of making the "quick buck" if the long run interests of the firm itself is not to be put at risk. Moreover, even in the short run, what is good for one firm in isolation may not be good for the business sector as a whole. The same message needs to be conveyed to practising managers also. Thus, the curricula for both the courses that turn out would-be managers and the executive development programmes that provide career development opportunities to in-service managers need to be re-oriented appropriately. As things stand now, some management courses, especially the advanced ones, do mention the model of far-sighted entrepreneurship in the spirit of the great pioneers (such as the legendary Henry Ford) and the type considerations underlying the game of Prisoner's Dilemma that were discussed in Chapter 5. However, these matters and their importance in the context of the inequality-growth nexus should receive adequate emphasis at *all* levels of management education.

It is also worth clarifying that what is being suggested here does not have much to do with the matter of *business ethics*, a topic on which much has been written over the last few decades. (For recent references see, for instance, Bowers and Paine (2017), Cornuel et. al. (2022), Ghosal (2005), Mirvis (2021) and Silver (2023). Older contributions include Frey (1997) and Singer and Singer (1997)). The business ethics literature can be summarised as follows: a business firm that is concerned exclusively with profit maximisation will be motivated to do things that do not conform to ethical principles (such as not complying with tax laws, not bothering about disclosing full information about the products or the firm to the final consumers, making false claims about the products in advertisements, polluting the environment etc.). While unethical activities may boost profits temporarily, in the long run they are sure to damage the reputation of the company. There is also some evidence that workers employed by firms engaging in unethical behaviour do not get job satisfaction. Workers are human beings. They prefer to have a moral purpose in life. Money wages and other material benefits of employment are not their only concerns. Unethical firms, therefore, do not have happy workers. Hence, such firms have a high turnover rate of employment. People are always moving in and out of such firms. All this lowers labour productivity and, therefore, ultimately the rate of economic growth. If managers are sensitised to these matters, this will not only help the firms to boost their long-run profits but also make for a happier and more committed work force, thus increasing social well-being in the broad sense.

Although there does not seem to be enough evidence regarding the statistical significance of the productivity-reducing effects of unethical business practices in the context of countries such as India, the basic contentions of the business ethics literature can hardly be disputed. On the contrary, these should obviously be made a part of the curriculum of management education courses. What needs to be emphasised, however, is that the economic arguments that were used above for a reorientation of management education have little, if anything, to do with issues of ethics. While ethics is certainly an important social science and merits serious study in its own right, the present book is not a book either on ethics in general or on business ethics in particular. It is a book on economics. Its central concern is with the fact that if business decision-making does not pay attention to the role of business managers in dealing with the inequality-growth nexus, it is the *business interests* of the private sector of the economy that will suffer (both in the long run and in the short). In this connection, it may be noted that since the matter is related to the self-interest of business firms, albeit in a broad sense of the term, the task of sensitising would-be business managers to these matters by means of appropriate restructuring of management courses may turn out to be quite feasible. Business managers need only to be made aware of where the *true* economic interests of the business firms lie.

6.4.2 *The role of management associations*

Associations of business managers are in a position to make a positive contribution towards sensitising the business firms to the need for taking socially optimal actions in their own interests. In the advanced economies, there have been some encouraging developments in this regard in the recent past. The World Business Council for Sustainable Development (WBCSD) is an association of about 200 forward-thinking companies. The companies are represented on the council by their respective chief executive officers. The declared mission of WBCSD is "to accelerate the transition to a sustainable world by making more sustainable business more successful" and its vision is "to build a world where nine billion people are living well and within the boundaries of the planet by 2050". The organisation seeks to develop an "action plan to help businesses face the three critical challenges of climate, nature loss and mounting inequality"[7] (see WBCSD (2021)). While it is not clear whether the concern for inequality that has been expressed here derives from an ethical value judgement or from the type of economic effects of inequality that are the subject of this book, it is not of much relevance here since a reduction of inequality will have the desired economic consequences, no matter whether it is economics or ethics that plays the motivating role.

So far as environmental and social inequalities are concerned, there are many other instances of awareness of the need to achieve a more egalitarian world. A global platform of business managers called Shared Value is working for social change through business solutions. It refers to shared value as "a business discipline where companies use their core business to drive societal change and enhance their competitiveness".[8] Again, as per a survey of Australian business executives, about one-third of the interviewees expressed concern at the fact that by neglecting environmental issues the present generation of business decision-makers are shifting the economic cost of the necessary corrective actions onto future generations of consumers, thereby increasing *intergenerational* inequality. Altogether, many business managers' associations are now of the opinion that that "doing the right thing" socially also "makes good business sense", appealing to "the broad spectrum of corporate stakeholders"[9] (see (Lawrence (2022)).

The reason why the roles of *associations* like these are particularly significant is that, as we have explained in the previous chapters, it is the *collective* action of the business decision-makers that has any chance of success in the fight against inequality. As illustrated in the game of Prisoner's Dilemma, no *individual* decision-maker can be expected to take a *unilateral* action towards achieving a more equal world.

6.4.3 Investor groups

Investors can also play a very important role in inducing business decision-makers to pay attention to inequality-related issues. By an investor we shall mean any individual or institution that supplies capital to the business firms. In the case of public limited companies, the most important investors are the shareholders and the lenders (including the holders of bonds issued by the companies and the financial institutions that lend to them). For other producers, it is the individual and the institutional lenders that are the important investors. Shares and loans are examples of what are called *financial assets*. Needless to say, for very small producers, personal savings often constitute an important source of investible funds.

In modern economies, an individual investor very often takes the help of professional *asset managers* and keeps his or her investible resources with one or more such managers. An asset manager gives advice, for a fee, as to what should be the investor's portfolio of investment, that is, as to how much of the total invested amount kept in the custody of the asset manager should be held in the form of company shares, how much of it should go to bonds etc. They also advise on the subdivisions within each category of investment (i.e. on how many shares of which companies are to be bought and on the similar question for bonds).

Large investors such as banks and other financial institutions, however, often have their own asset management divisions. These institutions and the professional asset managers who manage other people's portfolios together are often referred to as the *financial players*. In any modern economy, the financial players constitute the most important source of investible resources for the producers. This, of course, is not to deny the fact there are also many individuals who invest relatively small amounts of money and manage their own portfolios. In the context of our present discussion, we use the word "investors" as the catch-all term that includes any individual or institution that supplies money to the producers of goods and services.

In the advanced countries, investors' organisations have recently taken a number of steps to make companies as well as governments pay attention to inequality-related issues that are important for investors. For instance, Principles of Responsible Investment (PRI), a network of investors supported by the United Nations, has played a very positive role in this context. The Investment Integration Project (TIIP), a research project aided by PRI, has emphasised that if the economic and social inequalities are ignored, the business firms as a group would be facing problems. This would jeopardise their profit performance and that, in turn, will adversely affect the rates of return earned on the investment portfolios of the members of the investor organisations because these portfolios consist mainly of the shares and bonds of the large firms. TIIP, therefore, has argued that inequality negatively impacts investment performance (i.e. the rate of return earned by investors) in the long term by changing the risks and opportunities that affect investors and by destabilising the financial system within which all investors have to operate (see TIIP (2018)). It has, in fact, been argued that it was a prolonged period of high-income inequality in the United States that caused the Global Financial Crisis of 2007. The disastrous effects of the financial crisis on the rate of economic growth are well-known.

Moreover, although, as we have discussed above, inequality and polarisation are different matters, data reveal that in the United States, these two have moved hand in hand. For instance, the same TIIP (2018) study notes the finding by McCarty et. al. (2016) that points towards "the lockstep growth of inequality in the United States, as measured by its Gini coefficient, and the increased polarization of voting in the US House of Representatives from 1947 to 2011". While these data relate to the US economy, similar polarisation trends have been observed in many other economies. We have already commented above on how polarisation in a society undermines the social trust which forms the basis of a vibrant economy. Ultimately, people's trust in the government, too, is undermined by polarisation. A 2021 survey by the Organisation for Economic Cooperation and Development (OECD) reports that only half of the people across OECD countries say they trust their national government. (See OECD (2021)). There is hardly any need to elaborate on how damaging this can be to an economy.

A notable contribution of investor organisations in this connection is their campaign for data transparency regarding the activities of the large companies. In view of the discussion in the preceding chapters and in Section 6.2 of this chapter, it is particularly important that information about what the large producers are doing in respect of wage and labour policies, supply chain management and choice of technology is easily available to the rest of the society. Experience shows that the compulsion, whether legal or moral, to reveal relevant data acts as a nudge to the companies towards taking socially desired actions in order to ensure that the revealed data do not bring them bad publicity. So far as wages and labour rights are concerned, a number of investor organisations have taken the initiative of persuading large companies to reveal relevant data. A platform called the Workforce Disclosure Initiative (WDI) "aims to have companies to produce standardised and detailed reporting across the whole of their employment footprint, including on how they navigate and identify risks both in their direct operations and throughout their supply chains". WDI also asks companies "to document how they use their leverage in business relationships to create decent work standards and to meet expectations relating to the payment of living wages, adequate training and robust occupational safety and health conditions, among other things" (TIIP (2018)). In a similar vein, the Human Capital Management Coalition (HCMC), a coalition of 25 institutional investors managing a total of 2.8 trillion US dollars of funds has petitioned the US Securities and Exchange Commission to mandate the disclosure by companies of their human capital management practices. HCMC also intends to develop specific metrics for measuring the performance of the companies in these respects. There are instances of similar actions by other investor organisations.

Such campaigns have already achieved a bit of success. In the specific matter of supply chain management, for instance, it is heartening to note that in the USA over the past few years there have been increasing calls for "transparency in the textile industry (clothing and footwear) across the supply chain" and that, in response to these calls, an increasing number of large companies have reported on their main suppliers (Lawrence (2022), 14). This type of action clearly helps in preventing the proliferation of the practice of cutting labour costs by outsourcing to outside establishments of smaller size where wages are lower and other benefits are absent. Moreover, there is a cascading effect on the producers to whom the work is outsourced. For instance, as reported in Lawrence (2022), the information that is now publicly available has led to some new legislations in the state of California that now ensure that all producers in the garment industry have to pay the legal minimum wage to workers (rather than paying them at piece rates).

Similar efforts on the part of investors to sensitise the business firms on the need to follow socially optimal labour policies can also be expected to mitigate the adverse labour market impacts of the emergence of the gig economy because it is the lack of opportunities of regular employment that forces people to accept gig jobs. There is no reason why firms (including the digital platforms) cannot share the benefits of technological progress with the workers rather than seeking to appropriate all of these benefits for the purpose of maximising short-run profits by minimising the wage bill. As was discussed in detail in the previous chapters, socially suboptimal policies hurt the business firms themselves, especially in the long run. At this point, it only needs to be underlined that such ill-advised policies would, for obvious reason, also hurt the interests of those who supply capital to the firms. Investors, thus, have every reason to keep up the type of efforts that have been reviewed in this subsection.

Needless to say, the investor groups have so far achieved only a limited amount of success in this regard. There is still a long way to go. Even in the United States, progress in this direction has been limited to only a few industries such as textiles and to only a few of the states of the country. The situation is similar even in the other advanced countries. However, at least a beginning has been made. As the old Chinese proverb goes, "everything is difficult at the beginning".

6.4.4 Need for investor activism in India

The reader must have noticed that all of the examples of investor actions aimed at the reduction of inequality mentioned in the previous subsection were drawn from the United States and other advanced economies. The reason is simple. In countries such as India, it seems that even a beginning in this respect is yet to be made. There has so far been hardly any instance of an investor organisation campaigning over the need to persuade large producers to address either the issue of inequality in general or any of the specific factors causing economic inequality such as labour policies and supply chain management.[10]

It may be thought that in the Indian context, the importance of investor campaigns in this context should not be overstressed. Unlike in the US economy, large private sector companies do not contribute the major part of either GDP or the total employment of labour in India. More importantly, asset managers constitute a much smaller part of the economy in India than in USA. Consequently, they (or their organisations) wield much less clout with the large producers or with government policy planners than their US counterparts.

While this argument may not be wholly off the mark, not too much should be read into it. Under the neoliberal economic policies of the government, it is the public sector of the Indian economy that is shrinking. This implies a corresponding increase in the importance of the private sector. Within the private sector, in turn, the large producers are important economic players. As already noted in the preceding chapters, the degree of market concentration in many industries in India remains relatively high to this day. We have also already discussed the rise of the fissured labour market and the gig economy in India in response to the outsourcing policies of large companies. Therefore, persuading large producers to report data relating to their roles in combatting inequality is as important a task in India as it is in the advanced economies. On the other hand, while Indian asset managers by themselves are yet to gain much clout with the companies or the regulating agencies, investors as a group (that includes other institutional investors such as banks as well as investors acting individually) can certainly assert themselves. Investors, after all, constitute the source of finance for firms. It may also be noted that the argument applies to all firms (including family-owned ones) that employ hired labour. For family-*operated* firms that do not do so, however, the question of social optimality of wage and employment policies does not arise. While these firms, too, need to finance their investments, investor actions of the type that we have discussed above would not have much relevance here so far as inequality-related issues are concerned. Such actions, however, can still have a bearing on *other* social aspects of firm behaviour (such as those relating to carbon emission and other environmental issues).

6.4.5 Need for a broader coalition: Government, the civil society and international agencies

It is also possible to harness a broader coalition of forces for the purpose of fighting economic and social inequalities. Again, some beginnings in this direction have been made in a number of countries. First of all, the government obviously can play an important role in this context. While we have refrained from discussing the role that the government's monetary and fiscal policies can play in reducing inequality since much as already been written on these topics, there are *other* types of actions that the government (or, more broadly, the state) can fruitfully take in this connection. We have already mentioned CSR-related legislations and have explained why this particular type of government intervention is unlikely to have much economic impact. But it would make a lot of difference if the investor organisations' demand for data transparency regarding the companies' labour and supply chain management policies and their environmental footprints (such as carbon emission) receives legislative support. There should be laws containing provisions that requires companies to file annual reports incorporating this type of information. Some countries already have such laws in place. For instance, so far as *employee relations* are concerned, it was way back in the late 1970s that France introduced legal provisions of this type (see TIIP (2018, 16)). Companies with 300 or more employees were required to fill out a *bilan social* (social balance sheet) describing their employee relations. This was mandatory and separate from any voluntary reports on CSR. These reports were to be made available to the employees, the trade unions and, in case of publicly listed companies, to shareholders. Therefore, these were also available to institutional and private investors and could be used by them for deciding which companies to patronise in their investment portfolios. Since then, the mandatory social balance sheet has been introduced in several other European countries. This is a good template to follow. Obviously, however, it needs to be extended to include company policies with respect to supply chain policies also if it has to have economy-wide impact.

There is also the need to involve the civil society at large and the community of nations represented by such international organisations as the United Nations and its various arms. Some efforts at building such broader coalitions have also started. One promising start is the proposal to set up the Task Force on Inequality-related Financial Disclosures (TIFD). The idea was developed by two organisations, Predistribution Initiative and Rights CoLab. It was noted in 2020 that while their previously floated idea of the Task Force on Climate-related Financial Disclosures (TCFD) had received wide support and had already started work, there was the need for a similar initiative focusing on inequality (see Bauer et. al. (2020)). TIFD is a collaboration involving, among others, businesses, investors, financial regulators, policy-makers and academic experts. It emphasises that, like climate change caused by global warming, inequality also is a *systemic risk*, that is, that it puts at risk the entire production system of an economy rather than a particular business firm. Moreover, since all economies face this problem, it is a global phenomenon.[11] A strong point of the TIFD proposal is that it recognises that there is a two-way interaction between inequality and business firms. Firms have impact on inequality. This is described as the "inside-out" risk to the economic system. Conversely, there is the "outside-in" risk represented by the impact of inequality on business performance, a main focus of ours in this book.

TIFD aims at providing guidance, thresholds, targets and metrics for measuring both the "inside-out" and "outside-in" types of risks. Civil society and regulators as well as the business firms and investors can use the metrics to evaluate the private sector's performance. Currently, the plan is to develop usable metrics by the year 2025. Recently, the United Nations Development Programme (UNDP) and other organisations (for instance, the Argentine Network for International Cooperation and the Southern Centre for Inequality Studies) have joined the platform.[12]

6.5 The debate over "woke capitalism"

The previous section reviewed some of the steps that can be taken for the purpose of sensitising business managers about the need to be rational in a broad sense. It also noted that some (though not all) of these steps have started being taken in some (though not all) countries of the world although, even in those countries where a beginning has been made, there is still a long way to go.

Unfortunately, even the limited amount of success that has been achieved so far in this context has often been misinterpreted. Some critics have, in fact, opposed these steps. Recall that the focus here is on the need to reduce inequality and, therefore, on the need for every business firm to take into account the effects of its decisions on all stakeholders (i.e. all persons whose lives are affected by these decisions), rather than only the effects on its own shareholders. This has led the critics to apprehend that the efforts that have so far been made in some countries to achieve these objectives are actually parts of a leftist political agenda. Allegedly, the real intention behind these efforts is to replace capitalism (or, more specifically, the free enterprise system on which much of the philosophical foundation of capitalism rests) with socialism by nationalising the production units (or, at least, the larger ones among them) so that the government plays the role of the employer.[13]

In this connection, the critics have used the term "woke capitalism" to describe the reformed version of capitalism that engages with the various types of social inequalities. The term seems to have been coined by Douthat (2018) in a newspaper column and has been widely used in the media since then. The literal meaning of the word "woke" is not clear. The word does not seem to appear in the standard dictionaries (except as the past tense of the verb *wake* which does not give any clue as to what it means in the present context). Apparently, it is a colloquial African-American English word "that originally meant being alert to racial prejudice and discrimination but which is now used by the right as a catch-all insult for the political left and progressive causes" (see Caulcutt (2021)). The rightist critics of woke capitalism are particularly derisive of public relations campaigns by companies that seek to project a progressive image by flaunting their concern for historically marginalised racial or religious groups or for women and using these groups as mascots in advertisements with messages of empowerment. Basically, what these critics want is a return to "shareholder capitalism" where the sole concern of a business decision-maker is with the maximisation of the share values and, therefore, with the maximisation of the *current year's* profit of the particular firm. According to them, this is what will maximise social welfare. However, as discussed in Chapter 4, this claim is valid only under very stringent assumptions which are, more often than not, violated in reality. Rather, we agree with the view (held by the majority of experts) that traditional shareholder capitalism has led to a situation where inequality is at an unsustainably high level and the prospects of economic growth have been jeopardised. It is possible, however, to deal with both of these issues by bringing the interest of stakeholders into the picture (see, for instance, Collier et. al. (2021)).

Interestingly enough, woke capitalism has also drawn flaks from the political *left*. The leftist critique is that under this form of capitalism, the companies are more interested in improving their public image by *publicising* their concern for social causes than in taking effective steps for reducing inequality. It is argued that the only satisfactory way of solving the problem of economic stagnation that capitalism is presently beset with is to replace capitalism with socialism, thereby ending the process of exploitation of the workers. That is also the way to maximise social welfare.

It needs to be emphasised that the comparison of alternative economic systems (such as capitalism, socialism and various degrees of mixture of the two) from the viewpoint of social welfare is beyond the scope of this book. Irrespective of which type of economic system a country goes for, the basic argument of the book remains the same. Managerial decision-making must be *rational*. What *constitutes* rationality must, however, be appropriately defined.

6.6 Concluding remarks

The *leitmotif* running through the entire course of this book is that business decision-makers can (and, indeed, must) play a positive role in reducing economic inequality which is today one of the major constraints on the growth prospects of the global economy as a whole as well as of many countries in the developing world. Business firms need to share the economic prosperity endowed by technological progress with the rest of the society in general and with the workers in particular. The broad contours of such a plan should be clear. Some management experts have also given some specific suggestions. For instance, Govindarajan and Ramamurti (2015) mentioned that businesses should seek to provide (i) quality products at affordable prices, (ii) opportunities of gainful employment and (iii) access to services that would increase the productive potential of the people. These authors have also cited some instances of business firms in some of the emerging economies that have woken up to the need to reduce inequality by such actions. One hopes that the awareness spreads. Shared prosperity, as these authors remark, "is not about altruism or charity – it can be profitable in its own right". That also sums up the basic contention of this book. The book has only gone one step further by arguing that it is the *only* way to preserve both the profitability of the private business sector and the prospects of economic growth.

Notes

1 It has also been pointed out that the advanced countries of today have become advanced only by ignoring the problem of global warming and by relentlessly pursuing material growth. On this count, these countries have a moral responsibility of bearing the major part of any cost, monetary or otherwise, that has to be borne now to find a way out of the problem.
2 Because of this historical association, the word "Luddite" has now come to mean a person who opposes the use of any new technology.
3 As per the Oxford English Dictionary 2020, AI is "the theory and development of computer systems able to perform tasks that normally require human intelligence...". A sub-field of AI is *machine learning* (MI) which refers to "statistical techniques that enable computers and algorithms to learn, predict and perform tasks from large amounts of data without being explicitly programmed" (Acemoglu and Restrepo (2019)). AI, however, also refers to the ability of machines that can engage in visual perception, speech recognition, translation between languages and, most importantly from the viewpoint of this book, *decision-making*. The prediction aspect is also highlighted by Agrawal et. al. (2018) who emphasise that what AI in general and MI in particular basically do is to make it possible to make better and better predictions. It is this that enables computers to do many things that were previously done by human beings (for instance, fraud detection).
4 Conceptually, inequality and polarisation are different matters. Consider two persons Y and Z. Suppose that Y's income is higher than that of Z. Suppose, now, that there is an income transfer from Y to Z (so that their income gap decreases) but the incomes of all *other* individuals in the economy are left undisturbed. Suppose, furthermore, that magnitude of the transfer is such that Z's income does not become higher than that of Y after the transfer. This type of income transfer is called a Pigou–Dalton transfer. Inequality is defined to be what

decreases whenever there is a Pigou–Dalton transfer. Examples can be constructed to show that there may be a Pigou–Dalton transfer (which, by definition, reduces inequality) that *increases* polarisation. In principle, therefore, inequality and polarisation are different aspects of *inequity*. Note, however, that this does not mean that inequality and polarisation always move in opposite directions. In fact, the case that has been discussed in the text is one where they move in the same direction. Both increase.

5 This is most easily seen in the case of a firm in a perfectly competitive industry. Such a firm cannot influence the prices of either outputs or inputs. Suppose, for simplicity, that the firm employs only one input and produces only one commodity. Suppose that its production function is $q = f(s)$, where q is the amount of output and s is the amount of the input. The function f is a description of how or to what extent output changes when the amount of the input changes. Let p and w be, respectively, the prices of the output and the input. The firm's problem is to decide the amount of the input to be employed. It seeks to maximise profit which is $pf(s) - ws$. Whichever value of s maximises this expression is the amount of the input employed by the firm. Now, suppose that the parliament enacts a CSR law saying that each firm must spend a proportion α of its profit on social projects. Then, the firm will be interested in maximising its *net* profit which is $(1 - \alpha) [pf(s) - ws]$. Now, α is a positive constant. It is, however, less than 1 since no sensible CSR legislation would require firms to spend *all* of their profits on social activities. Thus, $(1 - \alpha)$ is constant and positive. It can be easily shown that presence of this positive constant in the profit expression will make no difference to the value of s that is chosen by the firm. Therefore, the level of output also will remain exactly the same as before. The argument can be generalised to the case of two or more inputs and also to the standard cases of imperfect competition.

6 In India, for instance, neither the rate of growth of GDP nor the rate of job creation in the private corporate sector registered an increase after CSR was mandated in 2014. The rate of growth actually declined between 2016–17 and 2019–20 (see Banerjee (2023)). The downward trend which continued in 2020–21 and 2021–22 can, of course, be ascribed to the economic crisis caused by the lockdown at the time of COVID-19. There was a recovery in the growth rate in 2022–23. Most observers, however, ascribe this to the combination of the effect of the pent-up consumer demand of the lockdown years and the windfall gain from the availability of cheap oil from Russia as an indirect consequence of the Ukraine War. The rate of corporate investment (as measured by gross fixed capital formation in the private corporate sector as percentage of GDP at current market prices), on the other hand, has registered an overall downward trend since 2014–15. Between that year and the last pre-COVID year 2019–20, this rate declined from 23.1 per cent to 22.1 per cent (see GOI (2023), Statistical Appendix, Table 1.9). In 2011–12, the rate was 27 per cent. The all-time high (27.5 per cent) was achieved in 2007–08 long before CSR came into the

picture. It seems difficult to be very enthusiastic about the macroeconomic effects of CSR.

7 The word "climate" here presumably refers to climate change which is a consequence of global warming and which is now known to have a wide range of adverse impacts including those on health and productivity. "Nature loss" refers to deforestation and degradation of the natural environment.

8 The name of the initiative, Shared Value, seems to be an interesting play on words to draw attention to the difference in approach from an exclusive concern with *share values*, that is, with the monetary benefits accruing to shareholders.

9 "Stakeholders" of a company include not only its shareholders but also anybody who is affected by the company's activities.

10 Some asset managers (such as mutual funds) are seen to issue newspaper advertisements from time to time exhorting everybody to be environment-friendly. The data transparency movement, however, does not seem to have progressed much in India.

11 Another reason, not noted in the proposal explicitly, why the problem is global is the fact that the countries are linked through international trade.

12 There is also a plan to integrate TIFD with the TSFD (which is an abbreviation for Task Force on Social-related Financial Disclosures), an idea floated by a different platform, Business for Inclusive Growth, that works with its strategic partner, the OECD. TSFD concentrates on the relation between business firms and social (rather than economic) inequalities. An integration of TIDF and TSDF would obviously enable both the business firms and the other decision-makers to work with a holistic conception of inequality. The idea of this integration is being supported by WBCSD. For further details about TIFD, see the website www.thetifd.org.

13 One possible source of this apprehension is the emphasis on the need to reduce inequality. In popular discourses, socialism is often identified with equality in the distribution of income and wealth. However, while, for obvious reasons, socialism is expected to reduce inequality, equality *per se* is not the *sine qua non* of socialism. Such an identification is, therefore, unwarranted. Socialism essentially means social (rather than private) ownership of the means of production. This is what sets it apart from capitalism. Whether the introduction of socialism will inevitably result in perfect equality of incomes and wealth is a different matter. On the other hand, there are countries (such as Sweden) that are not socialist in the technical sense of the term but display admirably low degrees of inequality in the distribution of income. If one must look for an agenda behind the policy recommendations of this book, it may be called *egalitarianism*. As has been mentioned more than once in the previous chapters, prescient economic thinkers as well as pioneering entrepreneurs have always been aware of the necessity of an egalitarian economy from the viewpoint of economic growth.

References

Abraham, K.G., Haltiwanger, J.C., Sandusky, K. and Spletzer, J.R. (2018): "Measuring the gig economy: Current knowledge and open issues", Working Paper No. 24950, National Bureau of Economic Research, Cambridge, MA.

Acemoglu, D. and Restrepo, P. (2019): "The wrong kind of AI? Artificial intelligence and the future of labour demand". *Cambridge Journal of Regions, Economy and Society*, Vol. 31, 25–35.

Agrawal, A., Gans, J. and Goldfarb, A. (2018): *Prediction Machines: The Simple Economics of Artificial Intelligence*, Harvard Business Review Press, Boston.

Banerjee, A.K. (2023): *Economic Slowdown in India: An Introductory Analysis*, Routledge, New Delhi.

Bauer, J., Rissman, P. and Rothenberg, D. (2020), "It is time for a task force on inequality-related financial disclosures", available at www.responsible-investor.com last accessed on August 22, 2023.

BCG. (2021): *Unlocking the Potential of the Gig Economy in India*, available at www.bcg.com last accessed on August 22, 2023.

Bowers, J.L. and Paine, L.S. (2017): "The error at the heart of corporate leadership", *Harvard Business Review*, Vol. 95, 50–60.

Caulcutt, C. (2021): "French education minister's anti-woke mission", *Politico*, August, 2021, www.politico.eu/article/macron-education-minister-jean-mitchel-blanquer-anti-woke/last accessed on August 22, 2023.

Collier, P., Coyle, D., Mayer, C. and Wolf, M. (2021): "Capitalism: What has gone wrong, what needs to change and how it can be fixed", *Oxford Review of Economic Policy*, Vol. 37, 637–649.

Cornuel, E., Thomas, H. and Wood, M. (eds.) (2022): *The Value & Purpose of Management Education*, Routledge, London.

Douthat, (2018), "The rise of woke capitalism", *The New York Times*, February 18.

Duggan, J., McDonnell, A., Sherman, U. and Carbery, R. (2021): *Work in the Gig Economy: A Research Overview*, Routledge, New York.

Frey, B. (1997): *Not Just for the Money*, Elgar, Cheltenham.

Ghosal, S. (2005): "Bad management theories are destroying good management practices", *Academy of Management Learning & Education*, Vol. 4, 75–91.

GOI. (2023): *Economic Survey 2022–23*, Government of India, New Delhi.

Govindarajan, V. and Ramamurti, R. (2015): "3 ways businesses are addressing inequality in emerging economies", *Harvard Business Review*, January, www.hbr.org last accessed on August 24, 2023.

IBEF. (2021): *Emergence of India's Gig Economy*, www.ibef.org/blogs/emergence-of-india-s-gig-economy last accessed on August 21, 2023.

Jensen, M.C. and Meckling, W.H. (1976): 'Theory of the firm: Managerial behavior, agency costs and ownership structure', *Journal of Financial Economics*, Vol. 3, 305–360.

Kuhn, K.M. and Maleki, A. (2017): 'Micro-entrepreneurs, dependent contractors and instaserfs: Understanding online labour platform workforces", *Academy of Management Perspectives*, Vol. 9, 157–162.

Lawrence, R. (2022): "Social inequality as a business risk", www.assets. kpmg.com/content/dam/kpmg/xx/pdf/2022/05/social-inequality-as-a-business-risk.pdf last accessed on August 15, 2023.

McCarty, N., Poole, K. and Rosenthal, H. (2016): *Polarized America: The Dance of Ideology and Unequal Riches*, MIT Press, Boston.

Mirvis, P.H. (2021): "From inequality to inclusive prosperity: The corporate role", *Organizational Dynamics*, Vol. 50, 10073, 1–10.

NSTC. (2016): *Preparing for the Future of Artificial Intelligence*, Office of Science and Technology Policy, National Science and Technology Council. Executive Office of the President of the United States, Washington DC.

NITI Aayog. (2022): *India's Booming Gig and Platform Economy: Perspectives and Recommendations on the Future of Work*, NITI Aayog, Government of India, New Delhi.

OECD (2021): *Trust in Government*, Organization for Economic Cooperation and Development, Paris available at www.oecd.org/governance/ trust-in-government/ last accessed on August 22, 2023.

Pant, J.J. and Majumdar, M.G. (2022): "Themes and narratives of gig economy: An Indian HR perspective", *NHRD Network Journal*, Vol. 15, 83–99.

Roubini, N. (2022): *Megathreats*, John Murray, London.

Sekharan, A. (2022): "India's gig workers: Overworked and underpaid", www.idronline.org/article/livelihoods/indias-gig-workers-overworked-and-underpaid last accessed on August 22, 2023.

Sengupta, R. (2020): *Entropy Law, Sustainability and the Third Industrial Revolution*, Oxford University Press, New Delhi.

Silver, D. (2023): "Meaningful work and purpose of the firm". *Journal of Business Ethics*, Vol. 185, 825–834.

Singer, A.E. and Singer, M.S. (1997): "Management science and business ethics", *Journal of Business Ethics*, Vol. 16, 385–395.

TIIP. (2018): *Why and How Investors Can Respond To Income Inequality*, The Investment Integration Project, New York, available at www.unpri. org/research/why-and-how-investors-can-respond-to-income-inequality/3777.article last accessed on August 22, 2023.

University of Bristol (2023): *Research reveals majority of gig workers are earning below minimum wage*, University of Bristol, Bristol, available at www.bristol.ac.uk/news/2023/may/gig-economy-worker-research.html last accessed on August 22, 2023.

WBCSD. (2021): *Time to Transform: Vision 2050*, World Business Council for Sustainable Development, Geneva.

Index